DIFFERENTIATION FOR EVERY CLASSROOM

Michael McDowell

Foreword by Tom Hierck

Michael McDowell, EdD
The Busy Teacher
Differentiation for Every Classroom

Published by:
FIRST Educational Resources, LLC
Winneconne, Wisconsin
www.firsteducation-us.com
info@firsteducation-us.com
ISBN: 978-1-7332390-4-2

Printed in the United States of America
(EnvisionInk Printing Solutions, Neenah, WI)

ABOUT THE AUTHOR

Michael McDowell, EdD, serves as the superintendent of the Ross School District. During his tenure, the Ross School District has progressed to the top of California districts in relation to student connectedness and well-being as well as being in the top tier of districts in academic achievement and growth. Beyond academic achievement and social and emotional development, the Ross School District has emerged as a beacon for innovation, creating 65+ different electives from virtual game design to broadcast journalism, and sponsoring the first TEDxYouth event in the Bay Area. This district is also in the process of creating a service-learning and community engagement program for all students to serve the local and global community.

Prior to serving as a superintendent, Dr. McDowell was an associate superintendent of instructional and personnel services and a high school principal of a Title I and California Distinguished School. Before entering administration, he was a leadership and instructional coach consulting with schools, districts, higher educational institutions, and state departments on educational leadership, teaching leadership, and instruction. Additionally, Dr. McDowell has several years of teaching experience in middle and high school science and mathematics.

Dr. McDowell serves as the chair of the Advisory Board for One Percent of Education, charged with facilitating leading experts in shaping a national narrative for advancing public education. Additionally, Dr. McDowell serves on the School of Environmental Leadership board tasked with scaling innovation in secondary school environments. Furthermore, he is CEO of Hinge Education, LLC, supporting professional learning in educational systems around the world. He is an international presenter, speaking on instruction, learning, leadership, and innovation. He is an author and consultant with Corwin Press, providing services in problem- and project-based learning, teaching and learning, systems and site leadership, and the Visible Learning Series. He is the author of Rigorous PBL by Design: Three Key Shifts for Developing Confident and Competent Learners (2017); The Lead Learner: Increasing Clarity, Coherence and Capacity for All (2018); Developing Student Expertise: A Guide for Ensuring Students Excel to High Levels of Achievement and Beyond (2019); and Teaching for Transfer: A Guide for Designing Learning With Real-World Application (2020).

Previously, Dr. McDowell was a National Faculty member for the Buck Institute of Education and an advisor to educational organizations focused on equity, excellence, and innovation. His practical expertise in schools and systems is complimented by his scholarly approach to leadership, learning, and instruction. He holds a BS, MA, and EdD and is currently completing course work at the Harvard Business School. He and his wife, Quinn, live in Northern California with their two children, Harper and Asher.

FOREWORD

Isabella is eleven years old and in grade 6. She enjoys school and does well at it by any traditional measure. When asked about what makes a difference in class and with her teachers, she indicates that she thinks everyone learns best when "teachers show us how, model with examples, and teach differently for each student to help them understand." Her favorite teachers use variety, games, and other adults (tutors) to help everyone learn. As expected with an eleven-year-old, she didn't use the word "differentiation," but it's clear to this educator that's what she was referring to.

So how do we ensure all teachers differentiate if it makes such a difference? How do we ensure that we have some common understanding of such a complex topic - one that has been bandied about in education for many years? Enter Dr. Michael McDowell with the text you are about to read. In the conclusion to the book McDowell says, "Teachers have the choice to make a significant difference in the lives of students." This is what Isabella was saying from the perspective she possesses, and it's the choice all educators need to process positively.

But where to begin? Look at these five questions and make note if you have pondered any (or possibly all) of them.

- I know I'm doing great things in my classroom, but are my students learning?
- When it comes to feedback, am I working harder than my students?
- Are our kids engaging in academic rigor?
- How do we get students to own their own learning?
- How can we collaborate to improve differentiation in our classrooms?

I know as an educator of almost four decades, all five questions have ebbed and flowed through my thought processes, and I'm not convinced that I have processed them through the lenses or the tools that my friend and colleague Dr. Michael McDowell has provided in this book. Knowing that educators need "something digestible and teacher friendly" when it comes to differentiation, he has written a book that not only provides strategies but also links, resources, videos, and protocols that colleagues can use as they try out the ideas presented (as indicated by the web icon throughout). To ground us all with a starting point, McDowell offers this definition:

Differentiation is a) teaching to the similarities of students along a continuum of learning and b) anchoring all student learning to a set of self and social management strategies that enable students to take responsibility for their own learning over time.

The five questions identified above frame each of the chapters, and Dr. McDowell shapes the work around student outcomes (those things students will demonstrate an understanding of) and teacher habits (actions that have a high probability of enhancing student competency at all three levels of learning) as he presents tangible learning opportunities for all educators regardless of their current level of familiarity with the work of differentiation. Many colleagues will be familiar with previous books written by Dr. McDowell and his simple taxonomy of learning across the levels of surface, deep, and transfer learning. When these levels are integrated, they form what he describes as rigorous learning. Combining this integration with the self and social management skills of orientation, activation, and collaboration provides the foundation for students to engage in academic success. Teachers providing the environment for this to occur forms the foundation of the work McDowell outlines in this book.

The choices colleagues make each day around instructional strategies to ensure their students have clarity, engage in quality feedback, and develop ownership of their learning model align with what every educator would identify as best practice. McDowell doesn't leave colleagues on the island of professional learning isolation but instead provides tangible practice that can be implemented on a daily basis. He shares an idea I often espouse to colleagues about focusing on your next, first step, make that step small and focused so you can progress forward. As he says in the book's conclusion, "Pick a key habit of practice. Then implement, refine, and inspect the impact of those habits on student learning. By doing this you will likely take the good things you are already doing and make them better and ultimately improve student learning." Isn't that the goal for all teachers, schools, and districts? Isn't that what Isabella said would make all the difference for her learning, and the learning of her classmates? Enjoy the text that follows and begin your journey with that next, first step.

Tom Hierck
Educational Consultant and Author
Husband, Father, Grandpa, Colleague, Friend and
Relentless Supporter of High Levels of Learning for ALL Students

CONTENTS

INTRODUCTION: MAKING DIFFERENTIATION HABITUAL

Let's face it—as educators, we are time poor and exhausted. Often, we are looking for quick wisdom for the next passing period, a potential new look into helping that one student we just didn't reach yesterday, and a few tools to freshen up our knowledge. We don't have the time for teacher conferences, the frustration that comes the day after the subs, or the challenge of taking in massive amounts of information in two days. We need something digestible and teacher-friendly. Plus, we all get the feeling that the people that present new information have no clue or don't remember the actual work of being a teacher. We need the five-hour energy drink of knowledge and skill. This book is written for you: the busy teacher.

This book offers practical guidance based on sound research. In addition, this book offers the type of professional development where the "shift happens" in our practice. Moreover, this book celebrates the great work you are already doing. Here is a book that is written from someone in the field who is doing the work right alongside you. If you are reading this, I imagine you have about eight minutes until the students come back from recess. You have guzzled down your water bottle and hopefully your sandwich in two bites. You are already frustrated by having to read these lines and want me to get on with it. Here we go!

Defining Differentiation

In season 4, episode 10 of Revisionist History, *The Obscure Virus Club*, the show's host Malcolm Gladwell asks David Baltimore what would have happened if the work behind understanding retroviruses had not been available at the time of the AIDS crisis. Mr. Baltimore answered, "Disaster." He went on to describe what happens to a society when the science behind an issue is unknown or the tools to solve a problem are out of reach. He remarked, "Not knowing what happens...gives liberty to fantasy."

Countless unknowns have paved the way for educators and school leaders to create fantasy solutions to the problems in education. A few resolutions that are frequently presented include: changing the size of a school or class, getting new teachers, and changing schedules. Countless pseudoscience approaches have wreaked havoc in education. Differentiation, a term that is usually considered the holy grail of teaching and learning, has not been immune to the fantasy movement in education. Unfortunately, we make this word out to be a big, hairy, audacious thing that no one can ever achieve. One reason is that educators often think we need to provide different activities for every single student and/or group. Often, differentiation is viewed as an approach that requires teachers to provide different instruction, resources, and support to every single student. This is wrongheaded.

Researchers have attempted to create grand theoretical frameworks and 27 step plans for differentiation that no human could master, understand, or implement. Pseudoscience has stepped up to lend a hand, offering "learning styles" to the mix of approaches teachers can use with students. I have to ask, how do you teach a kinesthetic learner linear-equations, or the auditory learner who can simply listen to naming compounds using the IUPAC system? Differentiation isn't about separation, sorting, and selecting activities for each individual student. Differentiation is a) teaching to the similarities of students along a continuum of learning and b) anchoring all student learning to a set of self and social management strategies that enable students to take responsibility for their own learning over time. In a number of texts, including *Rigorous PBL by Design* (2017), *The Lead Learner (2018), Developing Expert Learners (2019),* and *Teaching for Transfer (2020),* a simple taxonomy of learning has been laid out. This taxonomy is built on extensive research (Biggs & Collins, 1982) and is feasible for students to use within their own understanding of their learning across levels of complexity (McDowell, 2019). These levels of learning include surface, deep, and transfer:

- **Surface**: I can define, list, or use facts and skills
- **Deep**: I can relate facts and/or skills
- **Transfer**: I can apply facts and or skills in multiple contexts

When these levels of learning are integrated, students are engaging in rigorous learning. One way to define rigor-learning is the intensity of instruction and the integration of each level of learning (i.e., surface, deep, and transfer) are equal. Beyond developing such complexity of learning through surface, deep, and transfer, students need to develop the skills to take responsibility for their own learning. These self and social management skills include:

- **Orientation**: I know what I'm learning, my current progress, and next steps to improve my learning
- **Activation**: I know how to handle setbacks, combat boredom, stay focused on what is in my control
- **Collaboration**: I know how to give and receive feedback, solve problems with others, and engage in dialogue and debates.

When combined, students are well suited for engaging in academic and real-world situations (Figure 0.1).

Figure 0.1 *Integrating Levels of Learning and Self and Social Management*

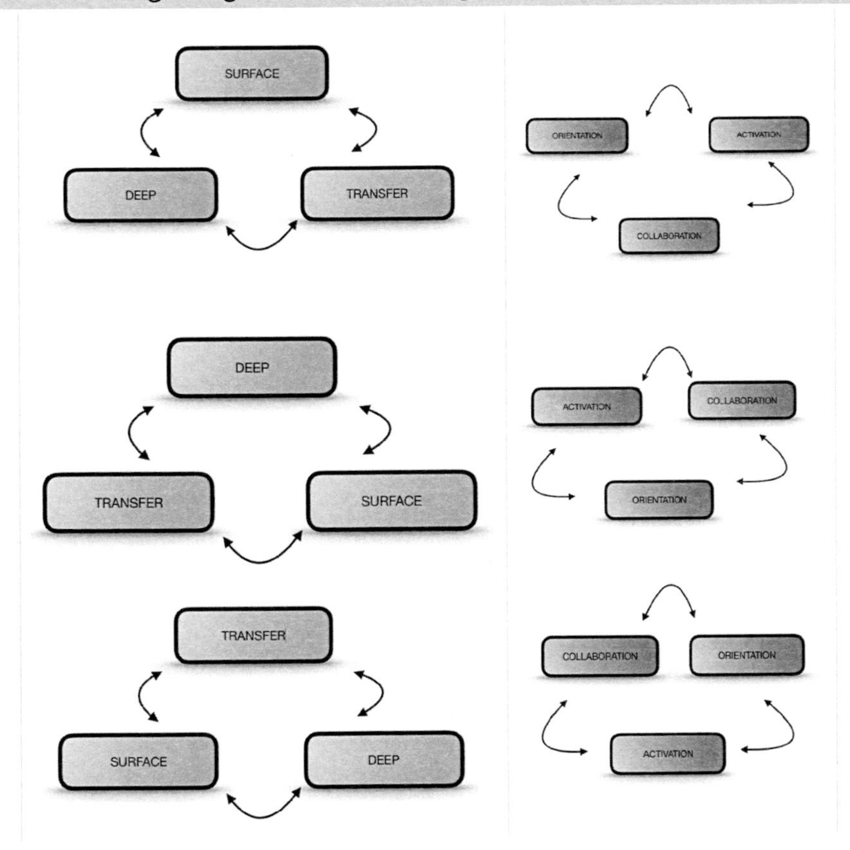

To ensure students integrate these knowledge and skills, we have to find ways to plan and execute daily practices that align with what every child needs at that moment. This requires a focus on core practices, or habits, that we can stick to each and every day. Gregory and Kuzmich (2014) argued that the right mindset for differentiation is helpful. The authors stated "a philosophy or mindset that enables educators to plan strategically in order to reach the needs of the diverse learners in classrooms today" (2014). They offered a set of beliefs that framed differentiation (see Table 0.1 below).

Table 0.1 *Beliefs Associated with Differentiation (Gregory & Kuzmich, 2014)*

- The mindset of teachers who are differentiating in their classrooms makes a difference.
- Students have diverse areas of strength.
- Students have areas that need to be strengthened and sustained.
- Each student's brain is as unique as his or her fingerprint.
- Learning possibilities are always present.
- Students bring their prior knowledge base and experience to the learning.
- Learning is affected by motions, feelings, and attitudes.
- Everyone can learn throughout life.

However, the best way to cultivate such beliefs is to focus on tangible daily habits. The formation and continued focus on implementation of such habits during classroom practice is the core purpose of this book.

'Doable' Via Habits

Habits may be best defined as routines, behaviors, or practices that are performed regularly. Habits reign in classrooms. As Wiliam (2019) stated,

> *because classrooms are such complex places, there really isn't time to think. Teaching involves continually making snap judgments about what to do next. Over time, teachers get better at reacting in ways that help their students, and these patterns of behavior get them through the day. Indeed, this ability to make the right call most of the time is a teacher's greatest asset. But it is also a liability, because the routines that teachers develop to do this are hard to change. (p. 172)*

Teachers are akin to race car drivers. The work is quick, becomes tacit, and every decision has massive implications and then you stick to those actions. As such, changing habits is incredibly hard to do, especially for teachers! Over time, habits are carried out without much conscious thinking of the behavior. Similar to driving a car or riding a bike, teaching often becomes a set of routines that we don't need to think about. When we do try a new practice, it is usually in a conference outside the context of the classroom. We rarely transfer this practice to the classroom when we get back.

Habit Change

Habit change is incredibly difficult to initiate and sustain. Firstly, we don't see the ideal results of our habit change for weeks, months, or sometimes years. In other words, there is a significant delay in meeting established outcomes as we build proficiency in new practices. Dave Brailsford, a successful coach and manager of the British National Team's cycling argued that the results of habits are "the aggregation of marginal gains." They have a monumental influence on outcomes over time. The delay does not feel good and we don't get the tangible results we want immediately (Clear, 2018).

This is compounded with the fact that we have been told countless times to focus on the goals of student achievement rather than focusing on our own specific habits of practice. In other words, we focus on the means to an end rather than seeing the means as an end in and of itself. Let's suppose you created a goal to change one of your feedback habits. You decide that you are not seeing balance in the amount of feedback you are giving in relationship to the amount of effort students are putting into using that feedback. You could certainly create a goal about increasing their feedback-guided effort, but that wouldn't change your means for increasing their effort. Instead, you decide to focus on your own feedback practices. You decide to shift your feedback practice in classroom discussions from a teacher-focused style (Type A) to a more student-focused style (Type B) (see Table 0.2).

Table 0.2 *Types of Responses to Student Learning*

Type A: Initiation- Response-Explanation	Type B: Initiation- Response-Response-Response-Consensus/Explanation
Colloquially "Ping Pong"	Colloquially "Basketball"
• Teachers asks a question by observing hands go up when prompted • Student responds with an answer • Teacher responds with the accuracy of the answer and provide a rationale for the correct response	• Teacher/Student asks a question via random • Student responds with an answer • Question is presented to another student (repeat) • Different answers from students are compared by students • Teacher asks for consensus and/or provides an explanation

You might be thinking, "Hey wait a minute. Why would I want to just focus on a habit rather than the outcome?" Well, research shows that when we focus more of our energy on enhancing our habits, we stick with them longer. So, you may well begin with an outcome (increase student effort from your feedback), but if you want to make a change, you have to center your interest on the habit (shifting the way you give feedback).

The purpose of this book is to give you a few key suggestions on how to maintain, develop, or remove habits of classroom practice that are linked to enhancing student learning for all students. Most of our professional development has been on practice outside of the context of students. This will not assist educators in changing our habits. As Wiliam (2019) argued, "It is much easier to change what teachers do when students are not present than it is to change what they do when students are present" (p. 171). Alas, teachers need help in changing habits in what they do on a daily basis *with* students.

Holding Onto Our Tools

New habits are difficult to develop because habits often feel integral to our identity. Habits are simple, reliable solutions to recurring problems in our environment. When we learn from others, especially those who have the same roles, we begin to form a professional identity around those habits. We have seen tools in all professions that align to a particular identity- togetherness in the military, using only quantitative data in launching space shuttles, using axes in firefighting, and, establishing and reinforcing classroom routines in education.

These habits have been built over time and have been overlearned. This is especially true in education, where most of us have been in the classroom since we were five years old. This phenomenon is called the *apprenticeship of observation*. Moreover, most teachers were successful in school and so they cling onto the habits their teachers used in the past (even if those habits didn't help other students). As such, teacher behaviors are largely independent of individual student learning. In fact, they are largely shaped on the cultural ideals of a busy classroom (Nuthall, 2005). Our habits, or tools, are based primarily on cultural traditions of teaching rather than learning and the nexus of the impact of learning from our teaching.

Dropping Good Tools for Better Ones

"Dropping one's tools is a proxy for unlearning, for adaptation, for flexibility " (Epstein, 2019, p. 226). In this book, I am not recommending that you drop every tool and habit. Remember, you are doing good things. In this text you may find a few new practices or habits to build and complement your practices. You may even decide to drop a tool and leave it there for a few years. None of the practices discussed in this book are going to cause an instantaneous shift in student achievement scores overnight. Over time, they will. This text suggests that when starting a new habit you follow the suggested process for at least six months before making alterations. Not an easy ask.

Next Steps

We are going to look at five questions, centered on key habits, that have a high probability of enhancing student competency at surface, deep, and transfer levels of learning and self and social management skills. Each chapter addresses one of the five questions. Each chapter includes a rationale for each practice, anchored by research, along with tangible examples and strategies for enhancing your practices and ultimately student outcomes.

Chapter Overview

Chapter 1: Creating routines for clarity in student learning	
I know I'm doing great things in my classroom, but are my students learning?	
Student Outcomes	**Teacher Habits**
Students will demonstrate an understanding of.... • learning expectations and ways to determine their current performance • different levels of mastery of knowledge and skill based expectations of learning.	Teachers will... • Engage students in discussions of successful examples in different contexts • Create knowledge rich learning intentions and leveled success criteria • Engage students in the co-construction of learning expectations and success criteria

Chapter 2: Making feedback mutual	
When it comes to feedback, am I working harder than my students?	
Student Outcomes	**Teacher Habits**
Students will demonstrate.... • how to use examples and assessment tools such as rubrics to assess their own work and that of others • strategies for giving and receiving feedback • discussing the actions they took or didn't take in light of feedback	Teachers will establish routines for students to... • develop accuracy in expectations of learning • self-assess and give each each other accurate feedback • Follow-through on feedback

Chapter 3: Ensuring Students Engage in Complex Work	
Are our kids engaging in academic rigor?	
Student Outcomes	**Teacher Habits**
Students will demonstrate.... • their level of understanding of surface, deep, and transfer through verbal articulation of their current performance and next steps they need to take • strategies they use to handle changes in tasks and changes in learning expectations across levels of complexity • their level of understanding of the pathway they are taking to learn surface, deep, and transfer	Teachers will... • Align instruction to all levels of learning (surface, deep, and transfer) knowledge and skill development • Engage students in changing expectations, situations, and perspectives. • Provide pathways for surface, deep, and transfer learning

Chapter 4: Establishing student ownership over their own learning	
How do we get students to own their own learning?	
Student Outcomes	**Teacher Habits**
Students will demonstrate.... • goal setting and planning next steps in light of performance data • their learning through multiple types of tasks • their knowledge and skill in working with others to develop shared understanding, to explore differing opinions, and to find solutions.	Teachers will.... • Ensure students are tracking their progress in learning over time • Provide multiple opportunities and choice for students to represent their understanding • Establish protocols for discussions, debate, and decision making

Chapter 5: Creating individual and collective efficacy: PLCs for Observable Impact	
How can we collaborate to improve differentiation in our classrooms?	
Student Outcomes	**Teacher Habits**
Students will demonstrate.... • a sustained focus on clarity, feedback, rigor, and ownership over their learning between and across grade level • iterative strategies for improving their learning by constant support from their entire teaching staff.	Teachers will.... • Create and monitor a plan of action for habit creation/elimination • Establish clear expectations of collective work • Script the critical moves of collective work • Monitor and improve team performance early and often.

Throughout this book, you will also see this icon indicating free links, resources, videos, and protocols that you can use as you try out ideas in this book. Just go to www.firsteducation-us.com/busyteacher, and you'll find everything you will need to make differentiation a reality in your classroom.

Pathway Forward

The outcomes and practices discussed in this book are certainly not exhaustive: They are a simple yet impactful set of expectations and habits that substantially move learning forward for students. It is important to remember that, as educators, we are doing great things for students.

Perhaps this book will give some guidance on how to continue to do great things, grow in a few other areas that leverage greater experiences and outcomes for kids, and perhaps let go of a few practices to enable us to do even better things in our busy professional lives.

Once practices are selected, we need to stick with or change certain daily habits in our practice. I bet most of you know what to do and how to do it, but it comes down to doing it every day for every student. Running once isn't super helpful for you. Exercising every day is a game changer. It is all about the aggregation of marginal gains. The rest of this book focuses on daily habits that make a difference for students. As you go through the rest of this book, ask yourself:

1. Which of these practices is realistic and doable for me in my context?
2. Which of these practices am I excited about trying?
3. Which of these practices am I willing to implement every day, with every class, for at least six months?
4. What will I do to remind myself of the need for this habit?

CREATING ROUTINES FOR CLARITY IN STUDENT LEARNING

The following chapter aims to answer the following question: *I know I'm doing great things in my classroom, but are my students learning?* By looking at research and walking through key teacher habits and practices (Table 1.1), you will be able to ensure that kids are with you as you are doing great things.

Table 1.1 *Student Outcomes and Teacher Practices*

Student Outcomes	Teacher Habits
Students will demonstrate an understanding of.... • learning expectations and ways to determine their current performance • different levels of mastery of knowledge and skill-based expectations of learning.	Teachers will... • Engage students in discussions of successful examples in different contexts • Create knowledge rich learning intentions and leveled success criteria • Engage students in the co-construction of learning intentions and success criteria

Looking to the Research

The aforementioned question stems from a substantial amount of literature that argued that the lives of children in a classroom may be completely, or almost completely, independent of the world of teaching. Graham Nuthall (2007) argued, "the busy classroom is not necessarily the learning classroom." In his years of research, he listened to kids who were recorded in classrooms. He found that kids were often not paying their utmost attention to teachers and were spending more of their time focusing on their peers and their peers' feedback (which was found to be mostly inaccurate) (Nuthall, 2007). Even more, Nuthall found that most of the classroom was hidden from teachers. His work implied that we, as teachers, can't see or hear what students are thinking. We also cannot know the subject or accuracy of what students are whispering to others.

Students are novices and as such simply do not think like experts (Willingham, 2009). Novices lack substantial background knowledge. Because of this, they glom onto familiar and concrete information and often miss, ignore, or oversimplify abstract concepts. Knowledge is like velcro, the more you know the more additional information will stick to your already learned knowledge. Even more, each student in our classrooms varies in the amount and strength of velcro (level of background knowledge and skill) and therefore experiences activities very differently. So, then what do students latch on to if they don't have the knowledge velcro they need?

Let's play this out. Pop quiz: What will kids remember out of these four items:

- Work in pairs
- Write three paragraphs
- Write a thesis
- Topic is cell phones in schools

My guess is they will remember bullet one (Work in pairs), bullet two ("write three paragraphs") and bullet four ("topic is cell phones in schools"). Working in pairs is a *work structure* and is a familiar behavior that students have experienced in school, sports, and at home. Writing three paragraphs is a typical *task requirement* that students are expected to do as a way to prove their competency in meeting the objective in bullet 3 ("write a thesis"). The topic of cell phones is the *context* in which students are learning content. They will assuredly have the mental Velcro needed for cell phones. More generally, work structure, tasks, and context are familiar and tangible to students. This is where novices focus their attention. This is why teachers, in large part, sometimes feel like we are repeating ourselves and become confused when students pay attention to certain instructions and not others.

Let's look at another example. What will kids remember out of these four items:

- Work independently
- Solve four problems
- Democrats, Republicans and Independent voters in Utah, California, Idaho, and Virgina
- Calculate percentages

My hunch is they will likely remember bullet 1 (work structure), bullet 2 (task requirements) and bullet 3 (problem context). "Human functioning relies on activating memory, rather than thinking. By nature, we try to avoid thinking but strive to solve problems by using our memories" (Hattie and Yates, 2014, p. 6). In the aforementioned example, students are activating their memories of procedures, facts, skills, and experiences that they have learned before. They will undoubtedly focus on their memory rather than actively think about calculating percentages, which is precisely our focus. Unfortunately, abstract concepts are what we usually want students to learn in school. They are certainly what standards are asking for.

There is another challenge that emerges for us while we are doing great things in the classroom. Research has shown that if students are not aware of their misconceptions and incomplete understanding, they will not pay attention to you and often will reinforce, or *double down*, on their prior knowledge (Muller, 2008). This is why Beers and Probst (2012) asked in *Notice and Note: Strategies for Close Reading* the fundamental question: "What challenged, changed, or confirmed what I already knew?" This may be why pre-assessments have more value to students than teachers. They need to know there is a gap in their learning. When we confound the hidden nature of the classroom, the challenges of the novice brain, and the peer influence of learning in the novice classroom, we find the complexity of the classroom to be simply breathtaking and overwhelming.

In a nutshell, here are three challenges that pull kids away from the great things you do:

1. The classroom is hidden, and kids give each other inaccurate feedback
2. Students tend to focus on the concrete elements of the classroom and not the standards to be learned, and

3. Students often don't pay attention while you teach because they think they already know the content and what they need to do.

Students need mental tripwires to pay attention to the most important factors of learning. For example, research illustrates that when students are clear on what they are learning and leverage *accurate* peer-to-peer feedback, student achievement skyrockets (Hattie, 2009). Teachers can create these tripwires by incorporating very tangible habits in the classroom to ensure students are with them when they teach. Let's look at three such practices.

Understanding the Practices

To ensure that students are cognitively engaged with you as you teach, we want students to demonstrate an understanding of learning expectations and ways to determine their current performance at different levels of mastery. For this to happen in our classrooms, teachers should consider implementing the following three habits:

- Engage students in discussions of successful examples in different contexts
- Create knowledge rich learning intentions and leveled success criteria
- Engage students in the co-construction of learning intentions and success criteria

We are going to explain each practice and provide examples along the way.

Practice 1: Engage Students in Discussions of Successful Examples in Different Contexts

Providing students with successful examples is an effective way to ensure students are clear on expectations and, as a result, can develop clarity of what is expected to learn. If we take a step back and think about ourselves, we will most likely agree that knowing what success looks like is a surefire way to get the outcomes we desire. The challenge is that we don't want students to fixate on the context, rely on the path of least resistance, or copy successful examples verbatim. The suggestion here is to give students a set of exemplars that are either (a) different levels of performance expectations that allow students to identify the typical progressions that they go through from initial drafting to a finished product or (b) different samples of ideal success in different contexts which allows students to identify the key criteria for success. This would make it less likely for them to get hung up on the context. Though examples may be used at any time of instruction, they are very helpful at the beginning of the learning sequence. They help students to develop the ability to know the goals of learning, to self-evaluate their current performance, and to plan out next steps to improve their own learning. As one second grader commented to me, learners need a "learning GPS."

To see a video of students using identifying their performance levels, go to www.firsteducation-us.com/busyteacher

Figure 1.1 *Example of Different Levels of Performance*

Examples of different levels of performance expectations

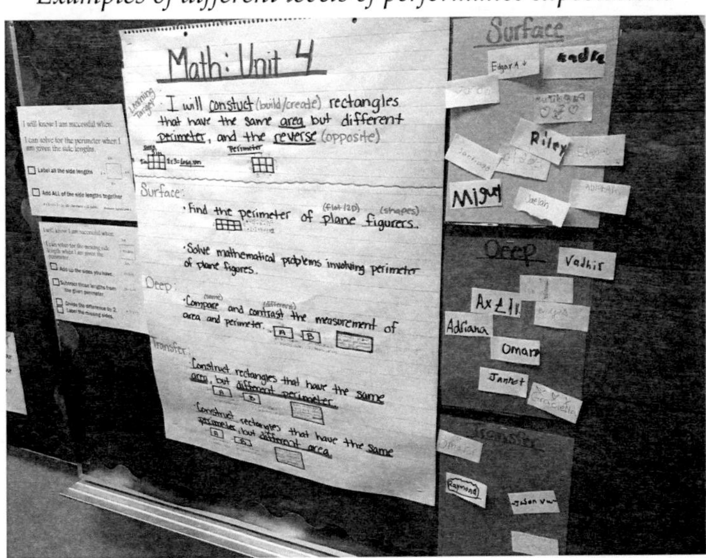

Palm Lane Elementary School, Phoenix AZ

Students need to know the destination, their current location, and the best route or routes to get to where they need to go. GPS is helpful when you start your journey. There are multiple ways to help students build a "learning GPS." Take, for example, the strategy of providing students with examples of success upfront. This allows students to interact with what success looks like during the unit of instruction. Moreover, it gives teachers an opportunity to pre-assess where students are in their performance and, as we will see later in this chapter, it provides an opportunity to co-construct expectations for student learning. This helps with increased clarity, accurately assessing their own work, and giving and receiving valid and reliable feedback.

Practice 2: Create Knowledge Rich Learning Intentions and Leveled Success Criteria

Willingham (2009) reminds us that we should think of to-be-learned material as answers to core questions. Our work is to take the time necessary to explain to students the questions. Each level of learning (surface, deep, and transfer learning) is primarily aligned to answering specific questions related to mastering and applying a learning goal (see Table 1.2). For instance, surface level expectations are typically the answers to "what" (fact-based knowledge) and "how" (procedural-based skills). Deep level learning is typically associated with answers to "why" questions. Students are typically looking for the relationships between ideas, representations of information, and the purpose behind decisions, formulas, and procedures. Transfer level learning is typically associated with finding the answers to questions related to applying knowledge and skills across different situations.

Table 1.2*Question Stems for Surface, Deep, and Transfer Expectations*

	Surface	Deep	Transfer
Question Stem Types	What? How?	Why?	When? Where? Should? Who?
Examples	What is a percentage? How do you calculate percentages?	Why is 100 the denominator of percentage problems? Why do we attempt to find 1% when solving percentage problems?	When are percentage calculations particularly misleading? Should percentages be used in all situations?

WHY LEVELED SUCCESS CRITERIA?

We define rigor students as developing their understanding and skills at all levels of complexity of core content knowledge and skills. We want to ensure that regardless of the class students attend, they are accessing facts and figures (i.e., Surface), relating those facts and figures into essential concepts and understandings (i.e., Deep), and relating those ideas into real world situations (i.e., Transfer). Leveled success criteria allows students to clearly see the different types of learning they are required to learn over time. Moreover, leveled success criteria provides teachers with a framing for expectations. As such, it may be deemed as an anticipatory activity for identifying next steps in instructional and feedback strategies to use at each level.

HOW DO STUDENTS USE LEVELED SUCCESS CRITERIA?

Students use surface, deep, and transfer as part of their language for understanding expectations, self-assessing and giving feedback, and determining next steps. The following video illustrates the power of leveled success criteria in understanding expectations, current performance, and next steps.

Let's take a look at an example of a learning intention and leveled success criteria. Figure 1.2 illustrates a learning intention which articulates the goal of learning for students. The learning intention should be written at surface, deep, or transfer level expectations. If the intention is written at the transfer level expectation, then the teacher needs to identify the key criteria at all levels of complexity for students to meet the established goal. If the goal is written at surface or deep, then the success criteria should be written up to those specific levels (i.e., surface and deep).

Figure 1.2 *Success Criteria Example*

Students need factual knowledge to utilize most of the skills we want them to develop during their academic life. The use of tools, such as number lines, Venn Diagrams, and Cornell notes, are all ineffective if students do not understand place value, key facts about a topic, or key words associated with details from a lecture or book. When creating learning intentions and success criteria, we need to ensure that there is balance between declarative and procedural knowledge. Examples of core academic knowledge include:

- Why is gravity constant and downward?
- To what extent does Algebra enable us to understand rates of change?
- Why does figurative language enhance readership?
- Examples of procedural knowledge include:
- How do you calculate a quadratic equation?
- How do I write a five-paragraph essay?
- Why is a number bond the best way to represent the relationship between multiples? Or if it isn't, why not?

Where should we include a variety of comparing and contrasting connectives in this passage?

To download a handout on procedural vs. declarative learning intentions and success criteria, go to www.firsteducation-us.com/busyteacher

To create a balanced approach to learning intentions, teachers can create declarative and procedural goals and criteria for students.

Practice 3: Engage in The Co-Construction of Learning Intentions and Success Criteria

The term *co-construction* refers to a process by which students work together to identify the success criteria that they will need to learn and be evaluated by over during a unit of study. Teachers at Santa Sophia Catholic College in New South Wales Australia have incorporated habits of co-construction of leveled success criteria with students.

To see a videos and documents of the four step construction process to develop leveled success criteria, go to www.firsteducation-us.com/busyteacher

Co-construction may be considered one of the most essential elements of developing student ownership over their own learning. Co-construction is the bridge between clarity of learning expectations, identifying current performance, and providing accurate feedback. Put differently, co-construction is a way to develop the "learning GPS." When implemented and engaged in correctly, students can answer the following three key questions:

- "Where are we going?"
- "Where are we now?"
- "What's next?"

To help students understand where they are going, there are multiple ways to involve them in discovering, understanding, and creating expectations of learning (i.e., co-construction). Those strategies include drafting and modifying criteria, deconstructing assessments, evaluating examples, error analysis, and silent procedures. For a detailed description of each strategy, please visit www.firsteducation-us.com/busyteacher.

Let's dive into one of those strategies here. When drafting and modifying criteria, teachers and students work through a series of steps to develop the success criteria for a set of learning goals (often used for procedural skills). The process is as follows: (a) Students are presented with a key learning intention (e.g., presenting an effective oral presentation), (b) students brainstorm success criteria related to a specific outcome (e.g., use stories), (c) students review selected teacher developed criteria (e.g., scan the audience), (d) students and teachers review exemplars to refine success criteria (e.g., TED talk, graduation speech) (e) students and teachers organize lists into leveled success criteria (students scan the audience while sharing stories that exemplifies the theme), and (f) students and teachers evaluate samples of work to refine success criteria and create consistency of assessing work (e.g., reevaluate TED talks watch new videos), and (g) students and teachers use finalized draft to assess, give feedback, and improve work (e.g., refine leveled success criteria).

Conclusion

The following chapter outlines three simple and powerful methods of differentiating our classroom routines to enhance student learning. As we will see in the next chapter, once expectations have been laid out, it is critical that we plan for instruction, feedback, and transfer tasks. We will look at strategies that enable students to answer the questions of "where are we now?" and "what's next?" Feedback lies at the intersection of these two questions.

Next Steps

1. Work with colleagues to identify key examples of success for your next unit of instruction. Then, draft learning intentions and success criteria that are

2. Embedded within the work examples. Finally, identify a particular method of co-construction of success criteria with students.

3. With your colleagues, determine the percentage of intentions and criteria that are written at higher levels of complexity (specifically deep and transfer) across a quarter of study/semester/year. Next, determine how many intentions are written for procedural-based skills vs. declarative knowledge. Discuss these percentages, wheth-

er this appears to strike the right level of rigor for students, and what steps the team needs to take to strike the right balance of declarative knowledge, procedural knowledge, and complexity of expectations (i.e., success criteria at surface, deep, and transfer levels of learning).

MAKING FEEDBACK MUTUAL

The following chapter aims to answer the following question: "When it comes to feedback, am I working harder than my students?" By looking at research and walking through key teacher habits and practices (Table 2.1), you will be able to see that students are working as hard or harder than you in their learning.

Table 2.1 *Student Outcomes vs. Teacher Habits*

Student Outcomes	Teacher Habits
Students will demonstrate.... • how to use examples and assessment tools such as rubrics to assess their own work and that of others • strategies for giving and receiving feedback • discussing the actions they took or didn't take in light of feedback	Teachers will establish routines for students to... • develop accuracy in expectations of learning • self-assess and give each each other accurate feedback • Follow-through on use of feedback

Looking to the Research

Let's do a time audit of your life during the school year. How much time are you spending at home assessing student work (pre or post COVID-19 pandemic)? 10 percent? 30 percent? 80 percent? Let's say that you work from about 7:30 a.m. to 4:30 p.m. each weekday. That's nine hours set aside for work and an estimated eight hours for sleeping. This gives you seven hours outside of those two events to live the rest of your life: exercise, commute, eat, watch Netflix, and feed, cloth, and bathe the kids. If you spend 10 percent of your time assessing work on any given day, you are using 2.4 hours per day on that rather than balancing other parts of your life. I think you should smell the roses!

Research supports my suggestion. Not just research on happiness and well-being, but research on student achievement. The most effective feedback is when students receive feedback when they are learning, which is almost always in the classroom. Moreover, most of the feedback kids get is from their friends and it's often wrong. We need to rethink feedback and make it more work for kids, in the classroom, and ensure that students are giving and using accurate feedback. Of course, the type of feedback matters just as much as the timing. Now, let's think about how many times we aim to be helpful to students by giving them answers or enough hints that they can answer the question without much (or any thinking). Students want you to give them the answer or at the very least enough hints that they can deconstruct your challenging problems to minimize thinking. As Hattie and Yates (2014) wrote,

> *. . . teachers are confronted with a roomful of students whose minds are designed not for thinking, but for saving themselves from needing to think. The thesis is not that students cannot think. It is that thinking in a 'school way' is not what comes naturally or happily for many individuals. Asking them to think about issues becomes an uncomfortable experience. But when it comes to complex learning and thinking, we err in assuming students will do so with enthusiasm and aplomb. Thinking means considering different perspectives. It means withholding impulses and avoiding making judgments in the absence of data. It means allowing evidence and research to overtake prejudice and opinion. It means an openness of mind to ideas that your students may never have encountered before (p. 9).*

The Trends in International Mathematics and Science Study (TIMMS) compared the types of math tasks students were engaged in around the world. They found some very interesting results. Regardless of where students went to school, they received a dose of both procedural and conceptual level tasks. Having said that, *substantial* differences occurred between high performing classrooms and low performing classrooms after conceptual problems were presented. Conceptual level questions did not survive the teacher-student interactions in the United States. That is, students never answered conceptual problems as presented. These questions were broken down into smaller, easier problems.

In one example, students were exploring variables for the first time. Through the interactions they had with their teacher, they were able to get the right answers to complete the worksheet and yet they didn't understand the actual math concept. How did they do this? The students engaged in a rapid-fire question asking process that, over time, the answers forthcoming from teachers transformed the deep level problem into a procedural problem. Once broken down, the students were essentially able to boil everything down to a binary (yes or no) response. The teacher mistook the multiple-choice game for productive exploration. Also, most researchers watching the teachers interact with students did too. The classroom looked active and engaged. If we remember from earlier, the busy classroom is not necessarily the learning classroom.

The classroom looked like it was progressing quickly in understanding mathematics. However, this was simply a knowledge mirage that quickly dissipated in the long run. Time and time again, videos of American classrooms showed students tackled zero conceptual problems. They didn't struggle to think. They found a way to avoid thinking and complete the tasks. Teachers were working hard but were also oblivious. In Japan, 50 percent of problems students engaged in were conceptual in nature and remained conceptual after they were presented to students. The students were required to struggle. As Epstein wrote, "excessive hint giving. . . produces misleading high levels of immediate mastery that will not survive the passage of substantial periods of time" (p. 89). You cannot retain something that you have not struggled with. This means that learning requires approaches to feedback and requires students to work towards answers without over-scaffolding their work. You simply can't hack learning, you have to work for it. Just like you can't hack a marathon--you have to run, a lot.

Understanding the Practices

Student Outcomes

Students will demonstrate:

- how to use examples and assessment tools such as rubrics to assess their own work and that of others
- strategies for giving and receiving feedback
- discussing the actions they took or didn't take in light of feedback

Teacher Habits

Teachers will establish routines for students to:

- develop accuracy in expectations of learning
- self-assess and give each other accurate feedback
- Follow-through on use of feedback

Practice 4: Establish Routines for Students to Develop Accuracy in Expectations of Learning

Over the past 18 months, teachers at Puebla Vista (a bilingual K-5 public school in Napa, CA) have made feedback an interactive process. In January of 2020, I dropped into a Kindergarten class and observed a teacher asking students to evaluate student work based on success criteria. Figure 2.1 illustrates the success criteria on the wall, four blank spots for students to position different pieces of work based on perceived levels of proficiency (1= red= not at surface learning, 2, yellow= surface level understanding, 3, green= deep level of learning, 4, green= transfer level of understanding), and the teacher holding up a piece of student work. The teacher presented a piece of work and asked students to determine, based on success criteria, its level of performance. Once students agreed on the level of performance, they had to talk with the teacher about why the piece met certain success criteria and why the piece failed to meet other criteria. Figures 2.1, 2.2, and 2.3 illustrate the teacher working with the students on determining performance of student work.

Figure 2.1 *Teacher Sample of Success Criteria*

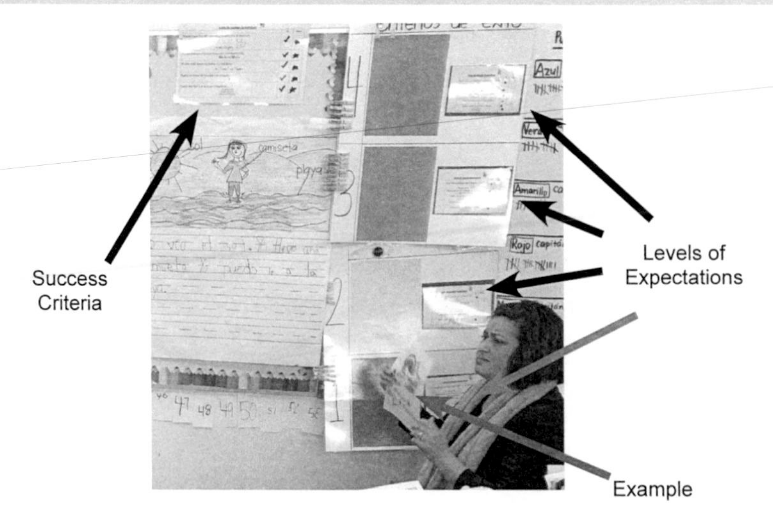

In Figure 2.1 the teacher is holding up a work sample and asking students to determine what level the sample meets in relation to success criteria. To meet the teacher's request, the students engage in a "Think, Pair, Share" process. First, students take time to individually determine what success criteria are included in the work sample. Second, students talk with one another about their evaluations of the piece. The teacher is listening in on the students' dialogue to assess their accuracy and use of success criteria to make their judgments. Finally, students share their insights (or that of their peers) on where the piece sits relative to expectations with the class and the teacher. This process is then repeated with subsequent pieces. Notice that Figure 2.3 shows one exemplar has been matched to level 1 (bottom red square next to the teacher). Now the students are looking at a new example and will repeat the think, pair, share activity. Subsequently, Figure 2.4 illustrates students publicly sharing their evaluation of the piece.

Figure 2.2 *Students Evaluating Their Work*

Figure 2.3 *Students Evaluating Their Work*

Let's look at the steps this teacher engaged in with the students:

- ❑ Reviewed Leveled Success Criteria with the students
- ❑ Provided work samples to the class
- ❑ Asked students to talk with their peers to determine the level of performance of the work example
- ❑ Had students share out with the rest of the class their opinions on the performance of the piece
- ❑ Asked clarifying questions to determine student thinking on their evaluation of piece
- ❑ Verified the accuracy of the students' evaluation of the piece
    - ❑ When there was a lack of accuracy, the teacher would refer to the success criteria and discuss evidence within the piece that either met or did not meet success criteria with students
- ❑ Repeated the steps with another piece of work

Figure 2.4 *Public Evaluation of Work Samples*

Overall, students see themselves as partners with teachers and each other in understanding expectations, sharing their ideas, and improving their work and that of others. I think that we often underestimate the level of interaction students need to be clear on expectations, their current performance, and the language and tools needed to give and receive feedback. Moreover, we often overestimate a student's ability to interpret and use teacher-based feedback and that of their friends. As such we need to make sure that students are with us. Let's take a look at another strategy for supporting students in giving and receiving feedback.

Practice 5: Establish Routines for Students to Self-Assess and Give Each Other Accurate Feedback

Once students have had direct practice using success criteria and student work samples to give and receive feedback, it is time for students to begin using those practices to evaluate their own work and that of their peers. Let's look at an example. Down the road from Puebla Vista at Shearer Elementary School, fourth grade students and teachers are actively learning how to ensure the feedback they are giving and receiving is accurate. Figure 2.5 shows the success criteria on the T.V. screen.

The teacher is providing instructions on how to give and receive feedback to peers' writing using leveled success criteria and examples.

Figure 2.5 *Success Criteria on the T.V. Screen*

Figures 2.6 and 2.7 *Success Criteria and Student Work*

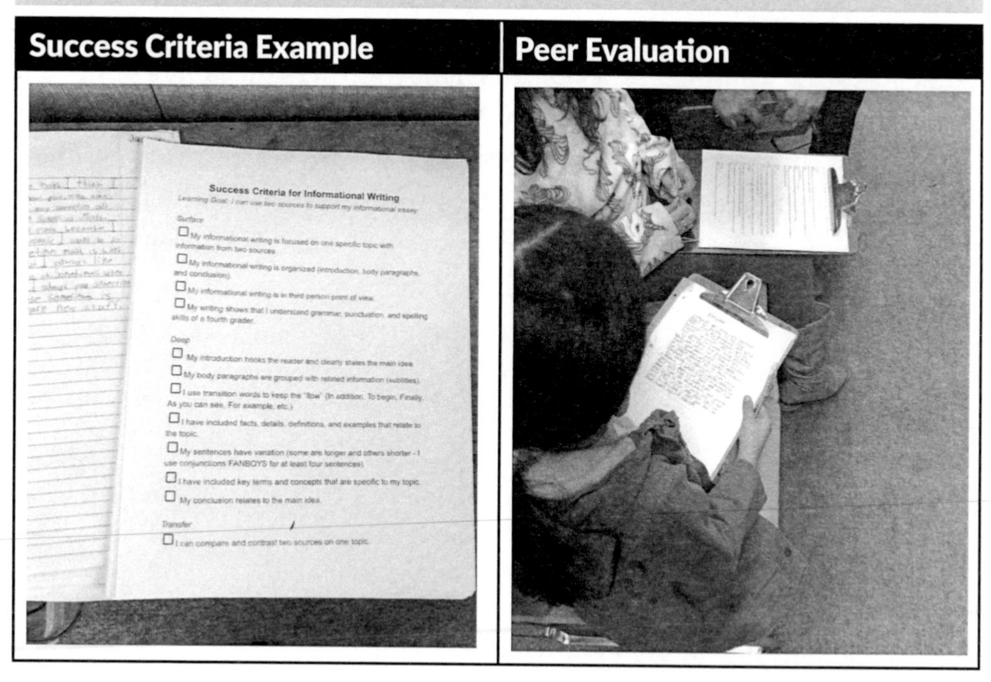

Figures 2.6 and 2.7 provide pictures of the leveled success criteria. In the photo, students are looking at each other's work to give and receive feedback. At the same time, on the other side of the world in New South Wales Australia, a kindergarten teacher walks an individual stu-

dent through the process of how to evaluate their own work. Here, the teacher is going through each of the success criteria with the student and asking him if he has met each one. The teacher is using questioning prompts to have the student think about prior learning, previous instruction, the work samples on the wall, and the success criteria to assess his own work. A key part of this process is for teachers to ensure students are using resources (success criteria, work samples, and their previous drafts) to reflect on their understanding of expectations, assess current performance, and to create next steps. Moreover, for students to share and incorporate feedback, routines must be put in place early and often. I have seen so many classrooms where the teachers and students invest significant time early on in a unit to clarify expectations and then not circle back to expectations, current performance, and drafting next steps. Clarity of learning (expectations, current performance, and next steps) is an *active* process. It requires regular reviews of performance and then must be followed by actionable *interactive* steps of both giving feedback and doing something with the feedback provided.

To initiate the process of establishing routines for students to self-assess and to give and receive accurate feedback, students should start with a set of diagnostic questions. These diagnostic questions include:

- "Where are you in your learning?"
- "How have you come to that determination?"
- "What are the expectations of learning?"
- "Where are you stuck?"
- "Where would you like feedback?"
- "Would you walk me through the success criteria you have met so far?"

One student I talked to walked me through where he needed feedback. In the following picture (Figure 2.8) you can see him pointing to the level four, or *transfer*, level expected piece of writing. In the discussion, I asked him where he was stuck and what next steps he needed to take. He referred to sample writing, the success criteria, and his own work while walking me through the "gap" in his learning.

Figure 2.8 *Success Criteria and Student Work*

When presenting these questions to students, teachers and peers want to ensure that they approach the work related to feedback with two key assumptions:

1. The person receiving the feedback should do the majority of the thinking, and
2. We don't know what the person receiving feedback is thinking.

To see a video of a student evaluating their work, go to www.firsteducation-us.com/busyteacher

When students are presenting their answers to the diagnostic questions, peers and teachers identify a strategy for capturing the information that is presented. A Gap Analysis is a fantastic strategy for framing diagnostic information (see Table 2.2). The protocol works by writing down the information first in the third column titled "Where are you going in your learning?" Here we are looking for students to discuss learning intentions, success criteria, work samples, and their current and previous work. Next, students discuss their current performance and why they believe they are at this level of performance. In the third step, students discuss what they think their next steps should be. Finally, the students state what feedback they are looking for to improve.

Table 2.2 *Gap Analysis Template*

Where am I now?	What's next?	Where are you going in your learning?
		• Learning Intention • Success Criteria • Work Examples

Table 2.3 *Gap Analysis Example*

Where am I now?	What's next?	Where are you going in your learning??
I have stated my point of view (POV).	My next steps include... Looking at various pieces of evidence that support my POV. Evaluating other POVs	The student will... Surface: state point of view Deep: relate supportive and counter- opinions with evidence Transfer: apply opinion writing structure to multiple contexts

When we give feedback we want to do two things:

1. Target feedback to surface, deep, and transfer levels.
2. Structure conversations so people are listening when they should listen and talk when they should talk.

Let's start with examples of giving targeted feedback. In the following example, we will be looking at two specific goals for a student (see Table 2.4 below). The first goal is linked to his ability to apply the singing of multiple notes in a song. The second goal is aligned to playing a string instrument. Now, let's imagine that we have a student that has just recorded a song on YouTube and has shared it with us to review and give him feedback. Go ahead and watch the following video: https://www.youtube.com/watch?v=ErMWX--UJZ4

Table 2.4 *Success Criteria for Singing and Playing a String Instrument*

Singing a song	Playing a string instrument
Surface: Sing one or more notes in tune (Doe, Ra, Mi) Deep: Sing multiple notes in tune and at different time sequences Transfer: apply words to notes at difference sequences of time	Surface: play a chord in tune Deep: play multiple cord Transfer: apply multiple cords in a song

After reviewing the video what success criteria did the student meet and what success criteria did the student not achieve? Here is how I evaluated the student on the success criteria:

Table 2.5 *Student Performance on Singing and Playing a String Instrument*

Singing	Playing a string instrument
Surface: Sing one or more notes in tune (Doe, Ra, Mi) Deep: Sing multiple notes in tune and at different time sequences Transfer: apply words to notes at difference sequences of time	Surface: play a chord in tune Deep: play multiple cord Transfer: apply multiple cords in a song

Next, we need to figure out how we want to give him the feedback that is just right for him, when he needs it. Because the student is at surface level learning in his singing, I would provide more direct feedback on the task of singing a note. I would say something to the effect of:

Step 1: Check on their own self-assessment: "Where do you think you are in your singing?

If they are struggling with their own self-assessment, then I would skip to Step 3.

Step 2: Check on their own thinking regarding their next steps: "What do you see as potential next steps to improve?"

Step 3: Give Feedback and Check for Action: "I noticed that you were missing many of the words to the song when you were singing. Because we want to apply our words to the song, let's start with making sure we know all of the words to the song. Go ahead and read them. Next, let's listen to the song and just hum the tune. Go ahead and hum."

Next, we need to figure out how we want to give him feedback on his Ukulele playing that will cause him to think. Because the student is at transfer level learning in his instrument playing, I would provide less direct feedback on the task and focus more on his own ability to self-monitor and advocate for what he specifically needs. I would say something like:

Step 1: Check on their own self-assessment: "Where do you think you are in your ukulele playing?"

Step 2: Check on their own thinking regarding their next steps: "What do you see as potential next steps to improve?"

Step 3: Give Feedback and Check for Action: "I wonder if you would re-watch the video with me, and we can pause the video every 15 or 20 seconds and discuss what you notice?"

Let's try one in English language arts. Table 2.6 shows an abbreviated list of success criteria for opinion writing and punctuation. Imagine we have a student that scores at the deep level in opinion writing and surface level for grammar. For deep level learning, I would start with the same approach I did with the ukulele playing. I would start by giving a student the opportunity to figure out the next steps, either individually or with others. With surface, I would still take an inquiry approach to begin my discussion with the student. Then, I would give more specific feedback and take a more directive approach in the expected actions.

Table 2.6 *Student Performance on Opinion Writing and Punctuation*

Opinion	Punctuation
The student will...	The student will....
Surface: state point of view	Surface: use sentences capitals in writing
Deep: relate supportive and counter-opinions with evidence	Deep: use sentences capitals in writing and for proper nouns
Transfer: apply opinion writing structure to multiple contexts	Transfer: apply across various types of writing

Table 2.7 *Surface and Deep Level Responses*

Deep Level Feedback Response	Surface Level Feedback Response
First, I would put students into small groups that had pieces of writing that were between deep and transfer level performance levels. Next, I would write down some feedback for each piece of work on an individual post-it note. **Step 1: Check on their own self-assessment:** I would go to the group and let the group know that I have provided feedback on individual post-it notes. The group needs to read all of the post-it notes and figure out which post-it note goes to which paper. They need to reach consensus on why they made the right selection and then they need to come up with specific feedback for each paper. **Step 2: Check on their own thinking regarding their next steps:** *What do you see as potential next steps to improve?* **Step 3: Give Feedback and Check for Action:** *I wonder if you would rewatch the video with me and we can pause the video every 15 or 20 seconds and discuss your thinking?*	**Step 1: Check on their own self-assessment:** I would ask students to swap papers with the person next to them and check their work to see if they met the success criteria. Next the students would talk with another regarding the assessment. **Step 2: Check on their own thinking regarding their next steps:** I would give students an example of a piece of work that has met all success criteria for grammar. Next I would ask the student to compare and contrast their work with the work sample and come up with potential next steps. If needed, I would provide more direct feedback. **Step 3: Give Feedback and Check for Action:** Look at the first sentence of your paragraph versus the example. What do you notice? Here is something I notice. I want you to correct that error throughout the paper. I will be back in 2 minutes to check on your progress.

OK, so what did we just do? First, we targeted feedback to each level of learning. When I was working with a student at the surface level in punctuation, I was more overt in sharing my thinking. For the student's opinion writing, I took a different approach. It involved looking at each other's papers, giving each other feedback, and constructing next steps. The commonality of all levels is that I used questioning to support students in thinking about their current learning against outcomes. When engaging in feedback conversations, it is incredibly helpful to ensure that they are structured in ways that make everyone feel safe and listened to. It's also important to allow for time to process information about how to improve. Table 2.8. illustrates several conversational frames that you may find useful when engaging in discussions related to feedback. Table 2.9 provides feedback frames at all levels of complexity (surface, deep, and transfer).

Table 2.8 *General Feedback Prompts*

Giving	Receiving
I notice that ...	I appreciate you noticing that ...
I wonder about ...	I hadn't thought about that ...
I was confused by ...	I heard you say that ____ confused you.
I suggest that ...	Based on your suggestion, I will ...
Have you thought about ...	Thank you, what would you do?
You might consider ...	I'm not sure what that looks like, tell me more.

Table 2.9 *Specific Feedback Prompts for All Levels of Complexity*

Surface	Deep	Transfer
I noticed that.... I wondered about... I was confused by... I suggest that.... Have you thought about.... You might consider....	What are the key similarities and differences between... Why did you use_____ suggestion? What was your reasoning for.... Why did you select this option as opposed to....	What do you notice about.... What are your key wonderings.... What are you confused by... What do you suggest.... What thoughts have emerged for you.... What might you consider....

Beyond feedback cues or prompts, structuring feedback through protocols is immensely helpful in routinizing feedback conversations. The *Charette Protocol* is one example of how students can give and receive feedback (Table 2.10).

Table 2.10 *Charette Protocol*

Charette Protocol	
Presentation of where you are going in your learning and where you are.	Presenter shares the following with a partner: • State your learning intention and success criteria • Present your work and discuss your current evaluation of the work against the success criteria. • What do you want feedback on.
Clarification	Partner asks clarifying questions. (ex. Could you please repeat how you met the following criteria?)
Feedback	Partner gives suggestions focusing on the specific thing the presenter wanted feedback on. Feedback is kind, helpful and specific. • I like... • I wonder... The presenter takes notes and remains SILENT
Discussion	Partner engages in specific next steps they will take and when they have those next steps accomplished.

Practice 6: Establish Routines for Students to Follow-Through on the Use of Feedback

Feedback is only impactful when it is used by the recipient. Teachers and students should create habits for checking in on progress *after* students receive feedback. Let's look at a couple of doable routines we can do in the classroom with students to ensure students do something with the feedback they receive. Table 2.11 and Table 2.12 provide strategies for ensuring students follow through on feedback received.

Table 2.11 *Trust but Verify Strategy*

	Description	Example
Who...	the person or group receiving feedback	A student received feedback that they confused RNA and DNA in terms of structure and function.
Does what...	The specific action	They were told to review the specific definitions, look up visual representations as well as provide examples of the function of each, and then self test
By when....	The timeline for accomplishment	They were told they had 15 minutes to conduct this review and would then share their key learning with the teacher.
Verified?	The means for checking on progress and completion	Two peers checked in every 5 minutes

Table 2.12 *30 sec/2 min/5 min Strategy*

When setting up a routine for giving feedback the following should be kept in mind:

- Frame feedback to key questions
- Engage students in a Gap Analysis
- Align feedback to surface,deep, and transfer
- Provide conversational prompts and protocols
- Create routines for checking in on action

I remember my daughter bringing home the following two drafts of her work from her second-grade classroom. I asked her why she had two copies of the same assignment. She said that her teacher had her compare these pieces and discuss how she improved in her learning after receiving feedback from her peers (see Figure 2.9). She told me that her peer told her she needed to add more descriptive language in her writing. She said that her peer asked her how she would describe horse riding? Then she said my daughter should include that description in her writing. My daughter said she went to work. After 5 minutes, the teacher asked my daughter to bring both drafts up to the front of the classroom and display them on the overhead. The teacher then asked my daughter to discuss the changes in her work and how the feedback she received moved her learning forward. I was awestruck by her reflections on her improvement.

Figure 2.9 *Pre-Post Student Work*

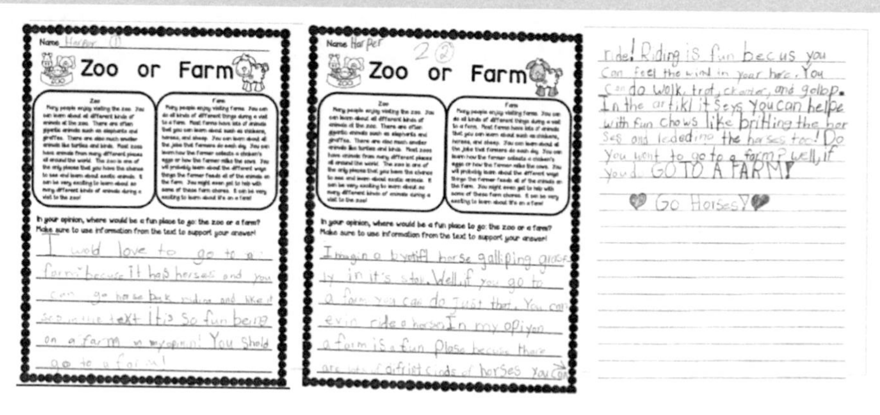

Reflecting on our actions with feedback is incredibly powerful. Let's look from students that discuss the power of using examples to improve their learning and that of their peers. At www.firsteducation-us.com/busyteacher you can find videos that illustrate students collectively practiced reflecting on criteria they didn't understand after an initial assessment. Students reflected on the reasons for their current performance and next steps they needed to take. This class took a step further and investigated the class performance before and after an assessment. One way to frame these discussions is through the use of protocols like the Charette Protocol mentioned earlier in this chapter, or other protocols discussed through the remainder of the book.

Conclusion

When the types of practices mentioned above are built into the habits of students' daily lives within and across school years, we begin to see accurate self-assessment along with clear, concise, and actionable peer to peer feedback. As such, students develop their ability to assess where they are going in their learning, their current performance, and next steps to improve. In current education research, this ability to self and peer assess has been deemed one of the most impactful strategies for improving student learning (Hattie, 2009; Wiliam, 2007). Moreover, through this process students and teachers begin to share the responsibility for feedback and improve learning for everyone.

Next Steps

1. Engage in a diagnostic assessment of the effectiveness of how well your students give, receive, and use feedback currently in your classroom. One tool that may be helpful in collecting this data is the following focus group protocol.

To see printouts for all of The Busy Teacher protocols, go to www.firsteducation-us.com/busyteacher

Focus Group Protocol:

Meet with a group of 4-5 students and ask the following questions. The questions include:

- How do you know that the feedback you are giving is accurate?
- How do you know the feedback you are receiving is accurate?
- What do you do with the feedback you receive?
- How do you feel about feedback?
- How do you work with others to solve problems together?
- How do you feel about being in teams or groups? Why?
- Are there any things that your peers could do to help you learn more?
- Are there any things that you could do to help your peers learn more?
- Can you tell me about a time when your peers really helped you learn something?

After collecting the data, reflect on the results with your colleagues and determine next steps. One way to engage in this discussion with colleagues is to use a charette protocol (see Table 2.9). Those steps may include having students evaluate work samples against the examples that you have posted on the walls. Another option would be to have students evaluate their own work and that of their friends against the examples on the walls. See some examples in Figures 2.10-2.12.

Figure 2.10 *Exemplars at Puebla Vista Elementary Napa, CA*

Figure 2.11 *Exemplars with Student self-appraisals at Napa Valley Language Academy*

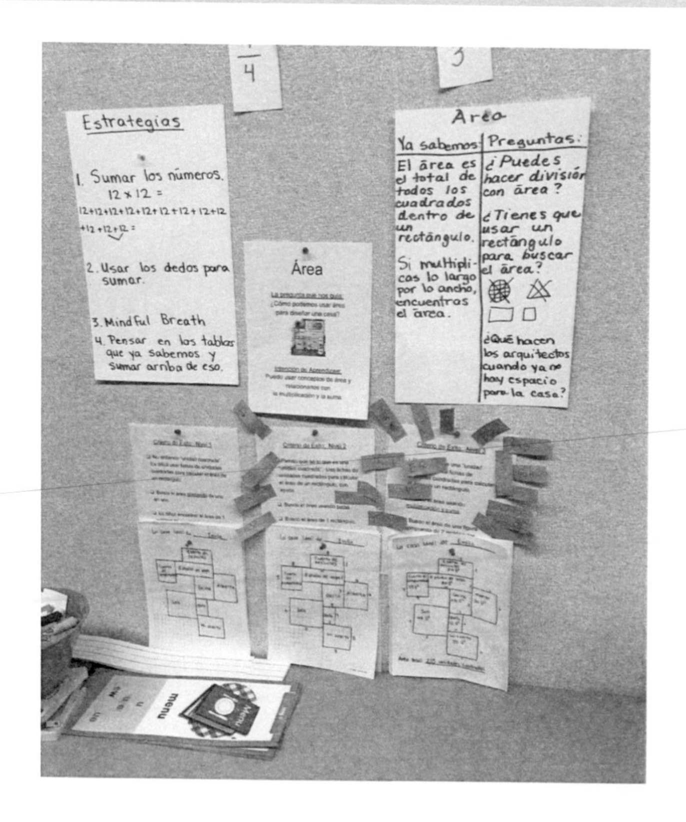

Figure 2.12 *Exemplars at Shearer Elementary*

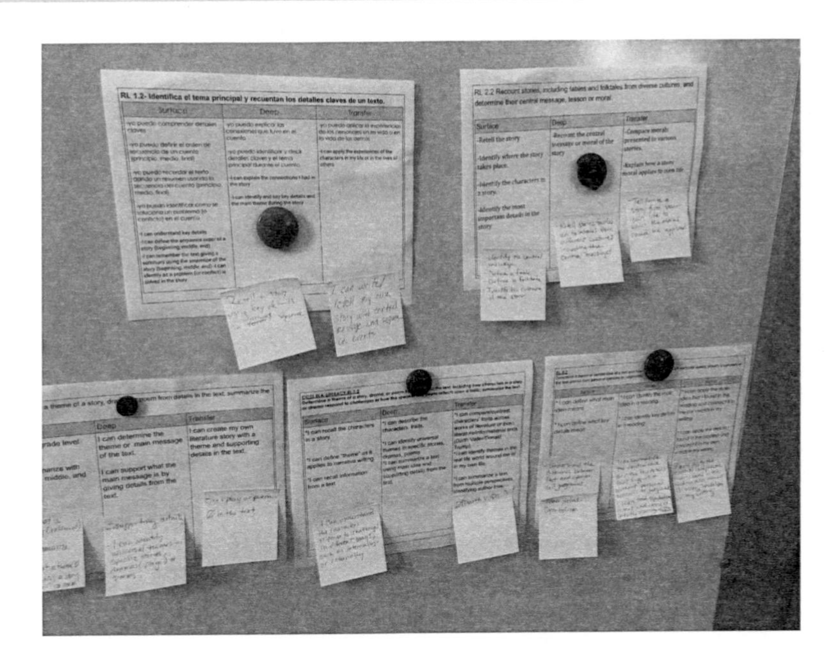

2. Before your next unit of study, provide your students learning intentions, success criteria, and work samples (see Figure 2.10 below). Go through the gap analysis activity with your class on expectations and current performance.

Figure 2.13 *Exemplar of Public Display of Learning Intentions, Success Criteria, and Student Work*

3. To refine the way you give feedback to students is to engage in a case study, pick one student at each of the levels of learning (i.e., one student at surface, one student at deep, and one student at transfer). Next, when providing feedback to each student, use the prompts discussed in this chapter. After one week, reflect on the difference in their growth and the changes in your own practices.
4. Implement one of the protocols (i.e., "Trust but Verify Strategy" or "30 sec/2 min/5 min Strategy") with students and reflect on the difference in students' behavior.

ENSURING STUDENTS ENGAGE IN COMPLEX WORK

The following chapter aims to answer the following question: Are our kids engaging in academic rigor? By looking at research and walking through key teacher habits (Table 3.1), you will be able to ensure that kids are engaging in rigorous learning experiences and developing core content knowledge and skills across surface, deep, and transfer levels of learning.

Table 3.1 *Student Outcomes vs. Teacher Habits*

Student Outcomes	Teacher Habits
Students will demonstrate.... • their level of understanding of surface, deep, and transfer through verbal articulation of their current performance and next steps they need to take • strategies they use to handle changes in tasks and changes in learning expectations across levels of complexity • their level of understanding of the pathway they are taking to learn surface, deep, and transfer	Teachers will... • Align instruction to all levels of learning (surface, deep, and transfer) knowledge and skill development • Engage students in changing expectations, situations, and perspectives. • Provide pathways for surface, deep, and transfer learning

In the figure below, there is a picture of two people. One is shoveling deep into the surface of the earth. He is determined, clear on his task, and is chasing the allure of reaching a light bulb moment. The other man is shoveling across the surface of the ground, illustrating breadth. He is searching for answers and chasing the allure of clarity. Which person is on the right path?

Figure 3.1 *Image of Surface, Deep, and Transfer Level Expectations*

The answer is both. Both are critical: The person shoveling on the left is a metaphor for developing depth in knowledge (surface, deep knowledge, and skills), whereas the person on the right is serving as a metaphor for breadth of knowledge (transfer knowledge and skill).

Rigor is the equal intensity of surface, deep, and transfer learning. They are of equal importance. Students need to have a thorough understanding and combination of knowledge and skills at surface, deep, and transfer levels. Students need to know facts and ideas, how to relate those facts and ideas, and how those facts and ideas apply in various contexts. For example, in physical education, students learn specific steps to implement defensive strategies in games (e.g., man-to-man and zone defense). Moreover, students link those defensive strategies to specific situations in a game (e.g., analyze offensive strategy from an opposing team in basketball). As students move towards transfer, they apply these skills and strategies across a variety of games (e.g., soccer, water polo, football). Students would then extend such strategies to contexts outside of physical education. They might be able to use these approaches in business sales, political strategy for elections, parenting, and immunology. The challenge is that in every class period, we face a classroom where students have specific learning needs that cross the surface, deep, and transfer continuum. We have students who have mastered core concepts and are looking for ways to deepen this understanding. We have other students that are ready to explore pathways across different contexts.

Santa Sophia College in New South Wales, Australia has worked to address this issue by establishing physical locations for students to meet in to learn at specific levels of complexity (see Figure 3.2). The picture below illustrates "hubs" where students engage in lessons that are aligned with the level of learning they require. As students enter each hub, they are provided with prompts on the wall for the types of feedback they are expected to give and receive, tasks they will address, and learning strategies that will support them in their learning (see Table 3.2).

Figure 3.2 *Surface, Deep, and Transfer Workshop Image: Santa Sophia Classroom*

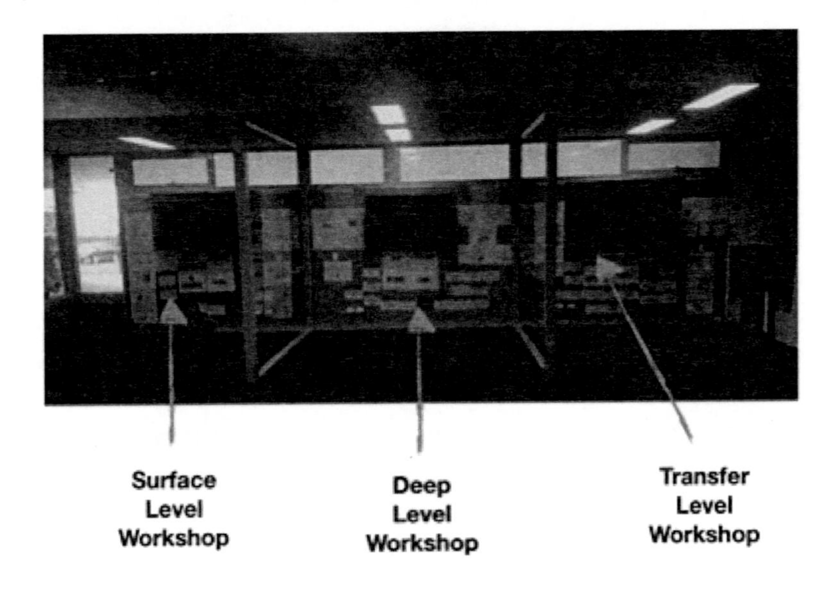

Table 3.2 *Feedback, Task, and Learning Strategies (Adopted from* **Developing Expert Learners** *McDowell, 2019)*

	Feedback Strategies	Tasks	Learning Strategies
Surface	• Is your answer correct/incorrect? • What is the correct answer? • Where did you go wrong? • What did you do well? • How can you elaborate on the answer? • Does your answer meet the success criteria?	Previewing new content (KWL, advanced organizer) Chunking content into "digestible bites" (e.g., The teacher presents content in smaller portions) Elaborating on new information (e.g., The teacher asks questions that require students to make and defend). Recording and representing knowledge	Outlining Mnemonics Summatiation Underlying and highlighting Note taking Deliberate practice Rehearsal
Deep	• What is wrong and why? • What strategies did you use? • What is the explanation for the correct answer? • What other questions can you ask about the task? • What are the relationships with other parts of the task?	• Self verbalization and self questioning • Evaluation and reflection • Using graphic organizers • Classrooms discussions • Seeking help from peers	Seeking help from peers Classroom discussion Evaluation and reflection Self-verbalization and self-questioning Metacognitive strategie
Transfer	Providing information to students that helps them self-regulate their learning by: Creating ways to self assess performance Strategies to seek support in learning Monitoring and investing in seeking and action on feedback to improve	Engaging students in cognitively complex tasks Creating analogies/ metaphors Evaluating multiple perspectives	Identifying similarities and differences in problems Seeing patterns in new situations

Within each hub, students are discussing the specific levels of learning they are in and what next steps they need to take to enhance their learning. On the Busy Teacher website, you will find two videos of students discussing their level of learning within the deep and transfer "hubs." In the first video, students are discussing the purpose of deep learning and their expectations for meeting deep level learning. Specifically, students are comparing and contrasting different human organ systems and discussing the enduring understanding of homeostasis within the human body.

To see the videos of the students discussing their learning, go to www.firsteducation-us.com/busyteacher

The second video illustrates a routine transfer level lesson. In this example, students are looking to apply their understanding of organ systems and homeostasis to real world scenarios, such as the impact of external environments (i.e., space, scuba diving at various depths) on the human body. All of the students are on the continuum of complexity (surface, deep, and transfer). Differentiation in this example helped students at their level of need. Often, we can differentiate student learning needs at surface, deep, and transfer levels when students are together. In fact, the most efficient way to differentiate is to teach the similarities in student prior knowledge. Consider classroom discussions: Teachers may assess their students' level of understanding. Based on that data, teachers may ask one student a surface level question whereas they may ask a different student a deep or transfer question (see Table 3.3).

Table 3.3 *Examples of Surface, Deep, and Transfer Discussion Questions*

Surface	Deep	Transfer
What is the definition of this term? What is an example (or a few examples) of the following definition?	I have just heard three key ideas, would you tell us how these ideas relate? Why are these ideas so important for the topic we are discussing?	Where would we see these principles in practice in our own discipline? Where else may we find these principles in practice?

Let's take a few minutes to look at the research behind *rigor* as the equal intensity and integration of surface, deep, and transfer knowledge. After we review the research, we will look at three key practices for ensuring students experience, engage, and learn rigorous academic content within and across disciplines.

Looking to the Research

The Case for Depth (Surface to Deep Learning)

When we think of rigor, we often think of the progressive pedagogies that are utilized at K-12 schools across Silicon Valley. We think of problem- and project- based and discovery learning as the bastion for bringing in rigor into the classroom through relevance. Unfortunately, this practice doesn't work in practice. At least not for novices. Novices, as discussed earlier, lack core content knowledge. As such, we are unable to operationalize the full potential of a methodology like problem and project-based learning (PBL). PBL is built for, and used by, experts. Don't buy it? The Organization for Economic Co-operation and Development (2016b and 2016c) found that inquiry-based instruction, including having students engage in experiments when they lack enough core content knowledge had a greater negative effect on student learning than missing school one day over a two week period.

> *Put bluntly, when students do experiments, they often do not have enough content knowledge to understand what they are seeing..... In fact, inquiry-based instruction had a greater negative impact on student achievement in science than student absence (defined as skipping at least one day of school in a two week period (p. 228).*

This is a difficult concept for experts to understand. Many people argue that skills are more important than knowledge in the 21st Century because we have access to technology and search engines. Many people believe that the ability to process information is more important than possessing information. Experts love the notion of devaluing knowledge in order to focus on building skill. However, experts already have knowledge. Because they utilize it so fluidly, they think it is their skill set that makes them successful.

However, experts' skill sets were built hand-in-hand with knowledge. That knowledge enhanced such skills. Experts have a revisionist history of what made them experts. They often overemphasize skills and deemphasize content. Doug Lemov stated, "When you grow up with knowledge...you can't really see the role of knowledge. The reverse knowledge gap for people on the privileged side of the achievement gap is that they have no idea how they got there" (Wexler, 2019). Many educators have this same belief. As Wexler argued, "The widespread belief among educators that history and non-hands-on science are inappropriate for young children isn't just at odds with what many parents sense intuitively. It's also not supported by the evidence" (2019, p. 28).

Let's look at an example of what all this means for kids. Here is a list of common comprehension skills:

- Summarizing
- Sequencing
- Inferencing
- Comparing and contrasting
- Drawing conclusions
- Self-questioning
- Problem-solving
- Relating background knowledge

Pick one of those skills and use it to comprehend the following passage:

> *Much depended on . . . the two overnight batsmen. But this duo perished either side of lunch – the latter a little unfortunate to be adjudged leg-before – and with Andrew Symonds, too, being shown the dreaded finger off an inside edge, the inevitable beckoned, bar the pyrotechnics of Michael Clarke and the ninth wicket. Clarke clinically cut and drove to 10 fours in a 134-ball 81, before he stepped out to Kumble to present an easy stumping to Mahendra Singh Dhoni.*

Now do the same with passage 2:

> *Churniak swings and hits a slow bouncing ball toward the shortstop, the passage began. Haley comes in, fields it, and throws to first, but too late. Churniak is on first with a single, Johnson stayed on third. The next batter is Whitcomb, the Cougars' left-fielder.*

Which of these passages were you able to effectively and efficiently use the skill you selected? Chances are, if you live in the United States, Passage 2 makes a lot of sense because you have prior knowledge of baseball. If, however, you were from the Southern Hemisphere or England, Passage 1 may be your selection because you have a background in cricket. This is completely independent of your reading comprehension skills. As Wexler (2019) argued, the implication is clear: abstract "reading ability" is largely a mirage constructed by reading tests. A student's ability to comprehend a text will vary depending on his familiarity with the subject. No degree of "skill" will help if he lacks the knowledge to understand it. There is a principle of cognitive science that runs counter to what many people have advocated in the 21st Century: "facts precede skills." Here is Wexler (2019) again: "The ability to think critically—like the ability to understand what you read—can't be taught directly and in the abstract. It's inextricably linked to how much knowledge you have about the situation at hand."

The other challenge is that skill development without emphasizing knowledge development may at first look like it is successful. In elementary school, students may test well with using developed skills, but over time, as the complexity of problems and the dependence of knowledge to understand contexts emerge, students begin to fail. There is a delay between the input and the results because there is simply less knowledge demanded in early elementary. As a result, assessments send false signals.

We want students to build knowledge by linking facts together into a coherent whole. This is what researchers call schema. A schema is like a map of a city. When students know the major landmarks and roadways as well as the directionality of the city, they are better able to solve problems (such driving from one place to another when there is construction). When students only know a set of facts (major landmarks) or a set of skills (using the index on a map), they are less able to handle situations (such as how to get from Point A to Point B). Recht and Leslie (1987) showed that prior knowledge was more important than comprehension skills. They stated that background knowledge is needed to learn most skills. Wiliam (2019) concurred, stating:

> *Practicing the skill of getting the main idea does not improve students' ability to identify the main idea of a passage of text very much, practicing problem solving does not improve problem solving very much unless there is a lot of knowledge stored in long term memory. (p. 150)*

Wiliam argued in his 2019 book *Creating the Schools Our Children Need,* that making progress in reading stems not from a lack of reading skills, but from a lack of knowledge in the content being read. He argued that solving math problems is not the way to learn to solve problems. The key, in fact, is ensuring students have a significant level of background knowledge to fluently find the main idea in reading and solving math problems (Wiliam, 2019). Knowledge reigns king in developing and teaching skills. Although skills are useful pointers, they should be presented and practiced but not to the degree that is required to build surface and deep knowledge.

Rigor is the equal intensity and integration of surface, deep and transfer of knowledge and skills. The crux of rigor is that often many students in our care need a significant amount of time to learn surface and deep knowledge. The approach to getting them there is through learning core academic content, developing skills through that process, and often intensive direct support by a teacher. As Wiliam argued:

> *For novices, worked examples--where they are taken through the steps of solving a problem by the teacher--are more effective than having the students solve problems themselves. For more expert students, problem solving tasks work well, because they have some spare capacity in short-term memory so cognitive load is not too great (p. 15).*

As such, students don't just need facts. They need to link facts and then use them. If you want children to think critically, they have to have something to think about. They need to have a thorough understanding of those ideas over time. They don't need knowledge that is a mile wide and an inch deep, but a mile wide and many feet deep. This has massive implications, not only on student academic achievement, but their ability to truly innovate in knowledge rich domains.

The Case for Breadth (Deep to Transfer Learning)

The ability to transfer knowledge begins with having well stocked shelves of content knowledge. Creativity is founded on our competence and the development of surface and deep level knowledge within and across domains. Students need opportunities, experiences, and specific instruction on how to transfer knowledge across different domains. As Epstein (2019) wrote, "modern work demands knowledge transfer: the ability to apply knowledge to new situations and different domains. (p. 45)"

Domingo, a computer programmer argued, "Knowledge is a double-edged sword. It allows you to do some things, but it also makes you blind to other things that you could do" (Epstein, 2019, p. 179). Unfortunately, most successful students are not given these opportunities, experiences, or skills to transfer knowledge across domains. When students with high GPA's in high school were admitted to the London School of Economics (LSE), they were compared to college juniors and seniors (Epstein, 2019). No difference in applying abstract concepts from a specific domain (i.e., economics, social and physical sciences) to common real-world problems was found between these students. In other words, students in high school or approaching graduation from LSE were no better at thinking critically when they came out of university than when they went in (Epstein, 2019).

The key to transfer is comparison. People must look *across* rather than *within*. *Widen* rather than *narrow*. *Open* rather than *close*. Study after study has shown that people fail to transfer learning across domains, even when they possess core knowledge and skills in different domains. This is because they fail to compare. Epstein (2019) cited an example using a student from Stanford's International Relations. The researchers presented two groups of students with a fictional scenario in which they had to find an appropriate response for how to support a small democratic country that was under threat from a neighboring totalitarian country. One group of students was given the following information: The president of the country was from New York, there were refugees in boxcars, and they were to meet in Winston Churchill hall.

The second group was told that the president of the country was from Texas and that refugees were in boats. Interestingly, the first group stated that the best strategy for the democratic country was to engage in war, whereas the second group believed that a diplomatic resolution was most appropriate. Both groups were subsumed with contextual information. The first group thought only of the World War II analogy whereas the second group thought of Vietnam. What if each group actually stepped out of their specific situation and analyzed different business ventures (e.g., potential monopoly), looked at different wars (e.g., Vietnam, WWII, and Iraq), animal behaviors (i.e., commensalism, mutualism, parasitism), and then determined a solution? Typically, people default to routine problem thinking rather than transfer level thinking (see Table 3.4).

Table 3.4 *Different Types of Thinking, From* **Teaching for Transfer** *(MCDowell, 2020)*

Surface and Deep Level Thinking	Transfer Level Thinking
• Focused on internal details of *one* situation. • When prompted, only look at comparison situations that are closely aligned with the situation at hand. • Overconfidence in one's own understanding of situation and rely on intuition and expertise within that situation • Determine solution and evaluate the problem later • Engage in "groupthink" with other experts	• Focus on similarities and differences between situations • Look at comparison situations that may have a distant relationship with the situation at hand • Use inquiry to test assumptions of one's own understanding of a situation • Start with problem types before jumping to solutions • Look at array of solutions before selecting a solution • Engage with others outside of areas of expertise

Students need to be able to pivot from ways of thinking that work well in a world of routines to a way of thinking that is required in a world of ill-defined problems. Students need new ways of thinking. The default is to double down on knowledge. Transfer is about leveraging breadth. Rigor is the combination of breadth and depth.

Epstein (2019) wrote that students need a Swiss Army Knife to "'dance across disciplines." However, one can't dance around disciplines if they don't have knowledge of those disciplines. Students need dollops of content rich knowledge. For example, the idea of teaching reading by teaching skills is, as Lemov (Wexler, 2019) stated, "a beautiful dream;" all you have to do is give kids a set of transferable techniques, and they can unlock any text and gain all the knowledge they want." It's a lot more compelling than, 'Actually, we have to teach all the details and facts and do all the legwork, and there is no shortcut." Lemov also stated, "It's a very seductive notion, the alternative to which is grueling hard work that a lot of people scorn" (Wexler, 2019)

Understanding the Practices

Student Outcomes:

Students will demonstrate...

- their level of understanding of surface, deep, and transfer through verbal articulation of their current performance and next steps they need to take
- strategies they use to handle changes in tasks and changes in learning expectations across levels of complexity
- their level of understanding of the pathway they are taking to learn surface, deep, and transfer

Teacher Habits:

Teachers will....

- Align instruction to all levels of learning (surface, deep, and transfer) knowledge and skill development
- Engage students in changing expectations, situations, and perspectives.
- Provide pathways for surface, deep, and transfer learning

Practice 7: Align Instruction to All Levels of Learning (Surface, Deep, and Transfer) Knowledge and Skill Development

As Kenny Rogers argued, "You have to know when to hold them and when to fold them." This lyric could not be more true when it comes to teaching and learning. Countless studies, over a number of decades, have shown that instruction and feedback practices are most effective when they are tailored to the learning needs of students (Hattie & Donoghue, 2016; Marzano, 2017). By learning needs, we are referring to surface, deep, and transfer learning. Research has shown that alignment of instructional and feedback strategies to surface, deep, and transfer learning is paramount to enhancing student learning (see Table 3.5). For example, when students are answering surface and deep level questions, direct instruction and specific targeted feedback on the accuracy of answers appears to be highly effective. These same strategies are less impactful at the deeper and transfer level learning.

Table 3.5 *Surface and Deep Instruction and Feedback Strategies (McDowell, 2019)*

	Surface	Deep	Transfer
Instructional Strategies	Direct Instruction KWL Chart Advanced Organizer	Jigsaw Venn Diagram Socratic Seminar Number Talks Pair-Share	• Engaging students in cognitively complex tasks (e.g., The teacher engages students in decision-making tasks, problem-solving tasks, and investigative tasks). • Providing resources and guidance (e.g., The teacher makes resources available).
Feedback Strategies	• Distinguish between correct and incorrect information • Prompt others to elaborate on information • Redirect others to paraphrase and offer examples	• Prompt others to articulate similarities and differences in concepts • Direct others to solve problems in multiple ways.	• Provide information to students that help them self-regulate their learning by – Creating ways to self assess – Strategies to seek support in learning – Monitoring and investing in seeking and acting on feedback to improve

Practice 8: Engage Students in Changing Expectations, Situations, and Perspectives.

Surface and deep learning is all about stable conditions of learning. The core focus here is for students to develop facts, ideas, and relationships amongst ideas and skills. The way in which a protein is made, the three branches of government, and the solution to a two-digit by two-digit multiplication problem remain the same. Transfer thinking (and doing) are focused on change and encountering non-routine situations. In *Teaching for Transfer* (2020), I discussed two terms: *perplexity* and *perspec-*

tive. Both of these are necessary for engaging students in transfer level work. Perplexity is associated with bringing in challenging dynamics to the situation. This may include changing the task on students, changing expectations of learning, or changing the task. Perspective is associated with looking at problems and situations from multiple angles. This may include the introduction of new tools to view a math problem or seeking the viewpoints of a vulnerable group in a specific situation. Table 3.6 walks through a few types of change that may be incorporated during the transfer learning phase of learning and instruction.

Table 3.6 *Adding Perplexity and Perspective in Learning from "Teaching for Transfer," McDowell (2020)*

	Description	Example I	Example II
Twists	Students are tasked with a change in success criteria requirements	Students are required to illustrate an additional contextual example within their work.	Students are required to include an interview from someone impacted by the situation.
Turns	Students face a new variable within a situation	Students are tasked with including changes in market given an embargo, natural disaster, or tariff	Students are tasked with including new polling data in their projections and recommendations for a political candidate.
Sequels	Students are provided with a new context within or after they completed transfer level work.	Students are tasked with looking at a new situation and discard the context they are currently evaluating	After the transfer level work is completed, students are required to apply their thinking to an entirely new situation
Multiple Perspectives	Students are tasked with finding different perspectives to a problem	Students are tasked with showing data in another form (from an algorithm to visual representations)	Students are tasked with reading texts from communities that are typically marginalized in the contexts being explored.

Practice 9: Provide Pathways for Surface, Deep, and Transfer Learning

Rigorous learning experiences involve surface, deep, and transfer level understanding and skill development. As such, teachers need to construct a pathway for students to experience all three levels of complexity (see Table 3.7). Pathway I offers the most traditional path. It starts students at surface level expectations and then moves to conceptual understanding (i.e., deep learning). After that process, students practice the application of knowledge and skills (i.e., transfer learning). Pathway II begins at the relationships between ideas, focusing students on the larger conceptual understanding of key content knowledge. Pathway III takes a more problem- or project-based approach. It starts at the application level and then works backwards through deep and surface knowledge to address application-based questions.

Table 3.7 *Three Pathways to Rigor*

Pathway	Description	Example
Pathway I: Surface > Deep > Transfer	The scope and sequence for students begins with learning surface level material followed by making connections between ideas, and then looking at transferring those ideas within and across contexts	Students are presented with the formation of proteins. Students learn about core definitions such as transcription, translation, and amino acids. Students are then put into groups and tasked with discussing the relationships between transcription and translation in the formation of proteins. Finally, students investigate an issue which has occurred within a cell that has caused an issue with protein synthesis. Students investigate the matter and present potential solutions and connect those solutions to potential analogous situations.

Pathway II: Deep > Surface > Transfer	The scope and sequence for students begins with exploring connections between ideas, and then looking at thoroughly understanding surface level knowledge and skills and then transferring those ideas within and across contexts	Students are presented with two questions, including Why do organelles work together? and Students then engage in surface level instruction. Students learn about core definitions such as transcription, translation, and amino acids. Students are then put into groups and discuss the relationships between transcription and translation in the formation of proteins. Finally, students investigate an issue which has occurred within a cell that has caused an issue with protein synthesis. Students investigate the matter and present potential solutions and connect those solutions to potential analogous situations.
Pathway III: Transfer > Surface > Deep > Transfer	The scope and sequence for students begins with attempting to transfer ideas within and across contexts. In order to accomplish transfer level expectations, students then work towards meeting surface and deep expectations (see Figure 3.3.)	Students are presented with causal chains and the importance of such a relationship in developing products including reviewing supply chains. Students then look at the relationships between building proteins. Students look at a challenging situation in which cells are manipulated preventing cells from engaging in their normal process. Students are then presented with information on how proteins are formed. Students learn about core definitions such as transcription, translation, and amino acids. Students are then put into groups and discuss the relationships between transcription and translation in the formation of proteins. Finally, they go back to their original problem and present their findings.

Conclusion

Differentiation begins by ensuring instruction and feedback are aligned to a student's need at surface, deep, and transfer level learning. Students need to know facts, procedures, and formulas that make up surface level knowledge. Direct instruction, guided practice, and corrective feedback are incredibly helpful for this type of learning. A student's ability to deepen their learning by establishing relationships amongst facts, know the purpose behind procedures, and critique formulas requires a different set of instructional and feedback strategies. These strategies are conversational, multifaceted, and, overall, less directive.

Transfer learning requires students to apply deep level learning across different domains. Deep learning is relating ideas, whereas transfer learning is relating situations to common ideas formed in deep learning. Strategies that best prepare students for transfer learning involve comparisons across contexts, handling change, and analyzing multiple perspectives. The use of comparisons is powerful to develop transfer level knowledge and skills. Developing multiple pathways to meet surface, deep, and transfer level expectations is key to ensuring that students meet rigorous expectations of learning.

Next Steps

1. Brainstorm a set of cues for students to refer to when working to learn core content knowledge and skills at surface, deep, and transfer levels. The following three figures illustrate examples that have been posted on the wall of a classroom to serve as gentle reminders for students to engage in each level of complexity.

Figure 3.3 *Surface Cues*

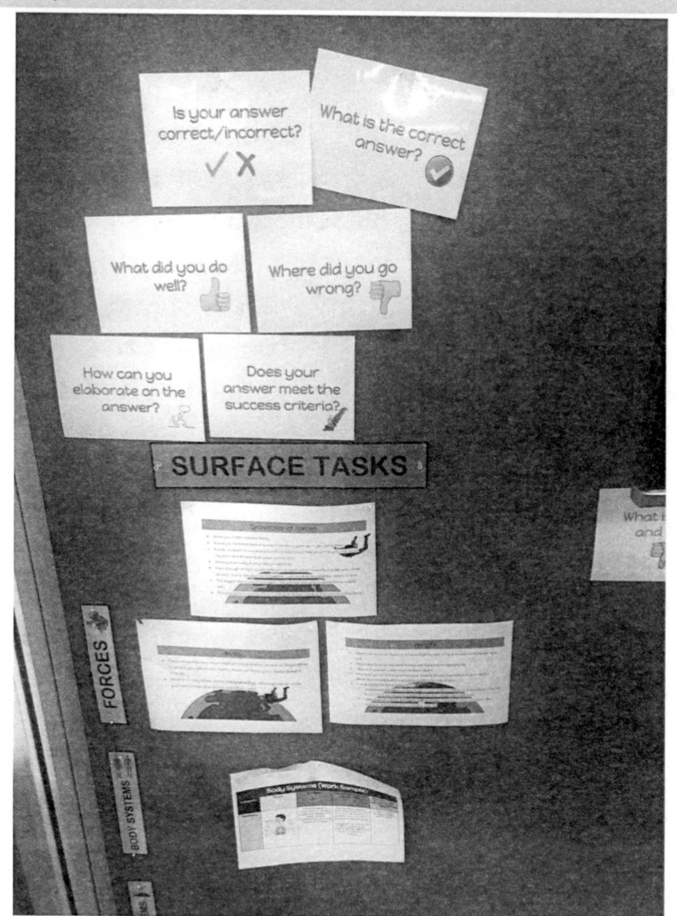

Figure 3.4 and 3.5 *Deep Cues Leveled Cues*

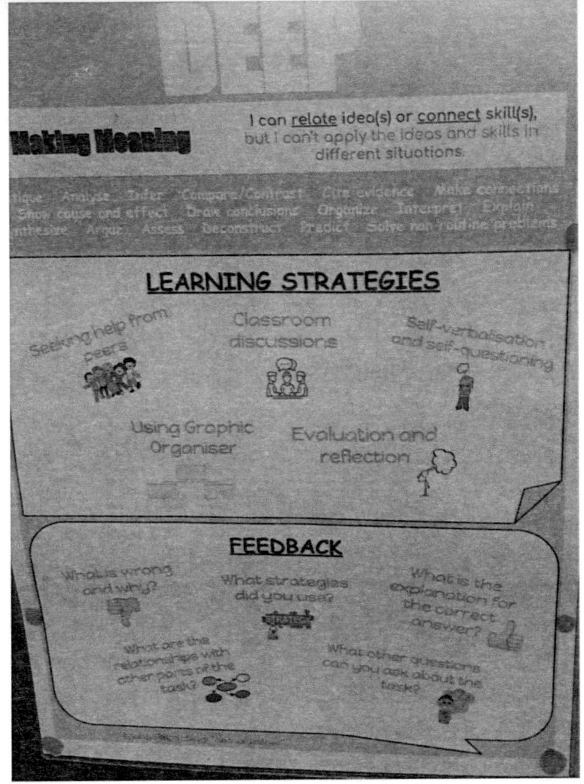

2. As a department, select a unit of instruction and brainstorm ways to ensure students are engaging in transfer level learning. Table 3.9 illustrates one way to frame these types of conversations.

Table 3.9 *Brainstorming a Process*

Brainstorm a change in the task....	Brainstorm a change in the criteria ...	Brainstorm a new context or change in how we view a context....
• Instead of submitting written paper you will need to provide a three minute presentation	• Instead of omitting current market trends and patterns you will need to include them in your analysis.	• Instead of arguing for gun control you will argue for greater personal freedoms as they relate to gun ownership or us (or) evaluate freedoms related to traveling during a pandemic.

3. In your grade level or department meetings, select a unit of instruction and develop potential pathways for ensuring students experience and learning surface, deep, and transfer success criteria.

ESTABLISHING STUDENT OWNERSHIP OVER THEIR OWN LEARNING

This chapter aims to answer the following question: "How do we get students to own their own learning?" By looking at research and walking through key teacher habits and practices (Table 4.1), you will be able to ensure that kids develop the skills to take ownership over their own learning.

Table 4.1 *How Do We Get Students to Own Their Own Learning?*

Student Outcomes	Teacher Habits
Students will demonstrate... • goal setting and planning next steps in light of performance data • their learning through multiple types of tasks • their knowledge and skill in working with others to develop shared understanding, to explore differing opinions, and to find solutions.	Teachers will... • Ensure students are tracking their progress in learning over time • Provide multiple opportunities and choice for students to represent their understanding • Establish protocols for discussions, debate, and decision making

Looking to the Research

One way of making differentiation a bit easier on everyone is to give students more ownership over their learning. Yet, as Table 4.2 shows, this has to be taught and assessed. Simply giving over control of learning to students in the classroom results in little to no learning. On the other hand, if we control their learning, students will be unable to take responsibility over their learning over time. They will likely be dependent on other teachers and people their whole lives. In reality, giving up control to students or taking control of students are two sides of the same coin. Students are rudderless without guidance and powerless with too much.

Table 4.2 *Student Ownership and Assessment Capabilities Comparisons Based off of* **Visible Learning Research** (*Hattie, 2009*).

Student Ownership over their own learning	Assessment Capabilities
Effect Size . 0.01	Effect Size 1.33
Equivalent no learning for the student	Equivalent Three or more years of academic growth.

Akin to swimming, they must be taught. Differentiation is not an innate skill, although we often think it is. We see children learn things without our direction. Ultimately, the human brain does do a few things well without much guidance. The brain survives well, recognizes emotions, and finds partnerships for mating. However, to learn complex abstract ideas and principles, the organ needs help! It needs teachers that offer the right balance of direction and autonomy (see Figure 4.1). As we discussed in Chapter 2, related to feedback, students and teachers need to find a mutual level of responsibility over learning.

Figure 4.1 *Continuum of Power in the Classroom*

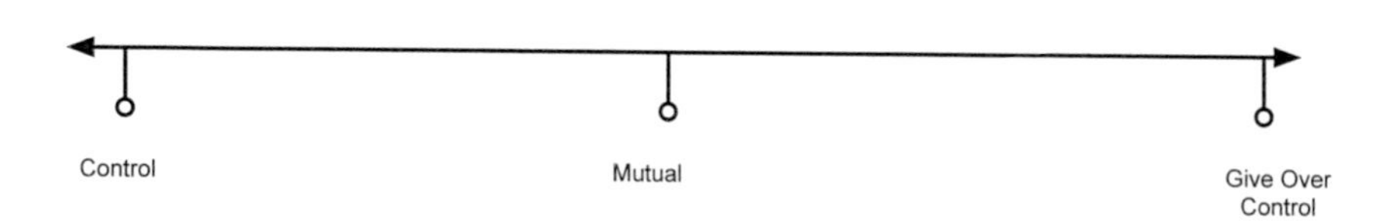

To develop ownership over learning, students need a set of specific skills. One of those skills, entitled *orientation*, is deemed as the most essential element of student learning. Think of orientation as a "Learning GPS" for students. That is, students know where they are going in their learning (i.e., their destination), recognizing their current performance (i.e., current location), and identifying next steps they yield substantial growth in their learning (i.e., the path they follow). When students develop this "Learning GPS," they are what research calls "assessment capable." They have the ability to assess their performance relative to outcomes and have a clear sense of steps they need to take to improve.

Figure 4.2 *Learning GPS*

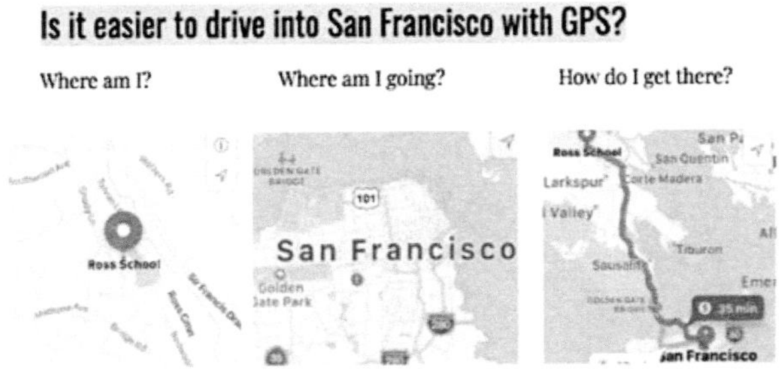

Is it easier to drive into San Francisco with GPS?

Where am I? Where am I going? How do I get there?

To better understand orientation, let's compare two scenarios in the classroom:

Scenario A: A student is writing an essay on the causes of the American Revolution. A teacher walks over and asks the student what she is learning. The student replies that they are learning about the causes of the American Revolution. The teacher then asks the student if they know where they are in the process of learning about the causes of the American Revolution. The student explains that she is trying to understand the concept of representation in government and that she is studying this concept by reading a short excerpt from her textbook.

Here is an example of what orientation doesn't look like:

Scenario B: A student is writing an essay on the causes of the American Revolution. A teacher walks over and asks the student what she is learning. The student replies that they are writing an essay that is due on Friday. The teacher then asks the student if they know where they are in their learning. The student explains that she has completed her outline and the first two paragraphs. She states that with a bit more time she will have the essay wrapped up this week.

Scenario A is focused on learning and the learning process whereas Scenario B articulates the specific tasks that need to be completed. If our students are spending the majority of their mental energy on getting things accomplished, then they are not working towards incorporating new information into their short term and long term memory. Kids, like adults, have due dates, but their mental energy needs to be on the quality of what they submit on those dates.

Temperature check

One quick and easy tool for determining if students are focused on what they are "learning" as compared to what they are "doing" is to ask students around the classroom the following questions: "Where are you going in your learning?" Where are you now in your learning?" and, "What's your next step?" If they articulate the goals of learning, the expectations for meeting those goals, and refer to successful examples they are typically focused on learning. As a result, put a tally mark under the learning category. However, if they focus on the activity they are working on, the tasks they need to complete, the roles and responsibilities of others , and/or the context, then they are focused on what they are doing. As a result, put a tally mark under the doing category. If they can articulate both what they are learning and what they are doing, then put a tally under the learning category.

Activation and collaboration are additional skills required for students to develop ownership over their own learning. Activation is related to the degree to which kids know how to handle setbacks, face boredom, handle doubt, and address misconceptions. One of the best ways of supporting students in developing activation is to have them focus on proactive steps to address failure rather than spending a significant amount of time analyzing the causes for failure. For example, one of the key skills of activating one's own learning is to conduct a self-assessment on their own performance and immediately focus on identifying next steps to improve. To develop this capacity, students go through a structured feedback process individually by evaluating their own work via success criteria and successful examples. Typically, protocols are used to evaluate student work (see The Busy Teacher website to download protocol templates). Teachers support this development by prompting students to evaluate multiple drafts over the course of the unit. This helps to determine their progress and proficiency. To ensure follow through, students would then share with others their growth, potential next steps, and clarify the support they need from peers, parents, and the teacher to continue to improve.

One tool to measure activation includes focus groups. In a focus group, a teacher, student, or administrator may select a small group of students (two to three) to meet and discuss a few of the questions found on www.firsteducation-us.com/busyteacher. After focus group data has been collected, the results are shared with the grade level, department, or at the school level to determine next steps.

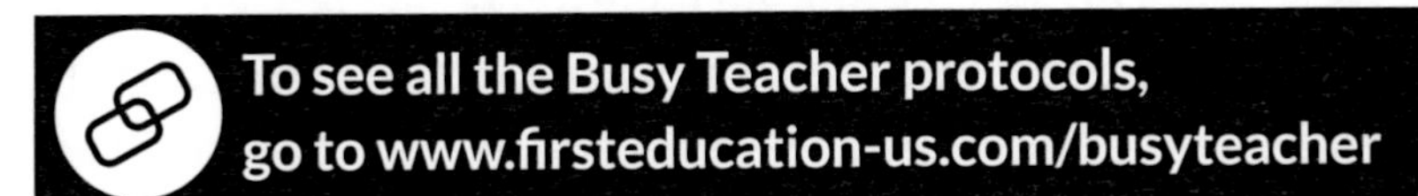

In the area of collaboration, we focus on children giving and receiving accurate feedback from one another, ensuring people share their opinions and listen to the opinions of others, and making sure that students collectively solve problems. This is certainly not an exhaustive list of collaborative skills, but common and critical key collaborative actions that have a substantial impact on student learning. To develop these collaborative skills, students should routinely give and receive feedback to/from their peers. One way to do this is for students to give structured feedback to other students by evaluating someone's work using success criteria and successful examples. Again, protocols can be used to evaluate student work . Teachers assist by prompting students to give and receive feedback with others during their unit of learning to enhance collective learning. At the conclusion of the feedback process, students discuss what next steps they are going to take. The teacher has students meet with peers that gave them feedback a week later to show and discuss the steps they have taken.

One tool to measure collaboration includes interviewing. In an interview, a teacher may generate a google form for a select group of students to answer a number of the questions. Once collected, the results are then shared with the grade level, department, or at the school level and next steps are determined (e.g., protocols to use when discussing data include *What?, So What?, Now What?,* and *In2Out*). Secondly, to develop these skills and establish mutual responsibility, students need emotional safety and support from their teachers. Students need to know that, not only do teachers know their subject matter and care about them as people, but that they are going to push them to meet subject matter expectations while supporting them emotionally when they are struggling to learn. Liking someone and having their back are two different things. A student needs to know that a teacher has their back and will support them to learn the material through their passion, high expectations, and scaffolding.

The difference between relationships with teachers and teacher credibility is subtle but substantial. Relating to someone on an emotional level, knowing they will care for you, and feeling supported is critical for learning. However, teachers must also push students to go beyond what students think they themselves are capable of becoming. Moreover, teachers must know their field and have passion for people learning it. Teacher credibility is about care with rigor. Teachers must have a passion for seeing students go beyond expectations. Another way to define teacher credibility is the degree to which teachers care deeply for students, their subject, and for students learning the subject. Credibility is when *passion* meets *purpose.* Here are recommended questions for showing your "street cred" to students:

1. Do students know you have their back?
2. Do students know that you are passionate about ensuring they learn your subject?
3. Do students know that you are competent in your subject?
4. Do students know that you have high expectations and will provide high support for them?

One tool to measure teacher credibility is to use the focus group and interview tools mentioned above. These tools illustrate suggested questions to ask students. Once collected, the results are then shared with the grade level and department teams. Then, next steps are determined to improve learning. In summary, teacher credibility, coupled with orientation, activation, and collaboration, must be partnered with a rigorous learning experience (surface, deep, and transfer).

Student metacognition is useless without being fully engaged cognitively. Imagine a coach telling a swimmer to control their breathing, hold their underwater streamline after the flip turn, and to think through the kicking. Now imagine that the student never had to engage in workouts that required this type of metacognition, especially while tired. This is often what happens when we think about "learning how to learn." We emphasize the thinking about thinking, but not the thinking when we are in the middle of learning. If we did this at regular intervals before, during, and after learning, students would have tangible, even visceral, evidence of their performance. Teaching students the skills of learning while learning knowledge is the key. Moreover, as in swimming, having a coach that believes in you, supports you, and moves you further than you expected in a catalyst for developing ownership over your learning.

Understanding the Practices

One way to start this work is to engage in the following three practices:

- Ensure students are tracking their progress in learning over time
- Provide multiple opportunities and choice for students to represent their understanding
- Establish protocols for discussions, debate, and dialogue

Practice 10: Ensure Students are Tracking Their Progress in Learning Over Time

For those of you reading this and wearing a Fitbit, there is a good chance you are going to feel a tiny vibration in your wrist if you don't start moving in the next few minutes. The Fitbit, one of hundreds of personalized electronic devices, are designed to enable you to track movement, sleep, heart rate, and calories. This information allows people to make informed decisions on their health that they otherwise would have done using intuition and anecdotal information. The level of knowledge gained from this tiny device gives us power and builds a sense of efficacy. What if we build a Fitbit for learners?

Students need similar information pertaining to their learning. We need to know our expectations of caloric intake and our current level of consumption to make an informed decision for what we eat later. Students need to know the expectations of learning, and their current level of understanding, so they can make informed decisions about what steps to take to improve. One of the best ways for students to build this sense of orientation is to set and monitor short- term and long- term learning goals. An important part of this process is designing a plan for monitoring such goals. For instance, students could take a short video recording on their year-long goals of learning. They could then engage in the same process midyear and at the end of the year. After making the video, the students could identify their current performance and write down next steps. You can see a video example at the Busy Teacher website. Here, a kindergartener shares that she is unable to read or write. She states that her goal is to read multiple sentences that she has written by the end of the year. In her video, she shows tangible evidence of her performance. In Figure 4.3, the kindergarten student illustrates her learning goals for the beginning of the year and discusses her progress over the course of a school year.

To see a video of the student showing the evidence of her performance, go to www.firsteducation-us.com/busyteacher

Figure 4.3 *Student Goal Setting and Progress*

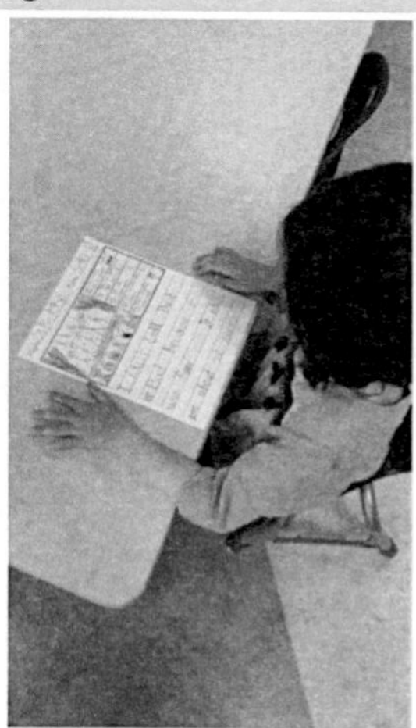

To support students in understanding and keeping track of their progress towards goals, it is helpful to have students evaluate their progress over time by looking at their work over time. Figure 4.4 shows students work from the beginning to the end of a unit of writing.

Figure 4.4 *Student Work Samples Over Time*

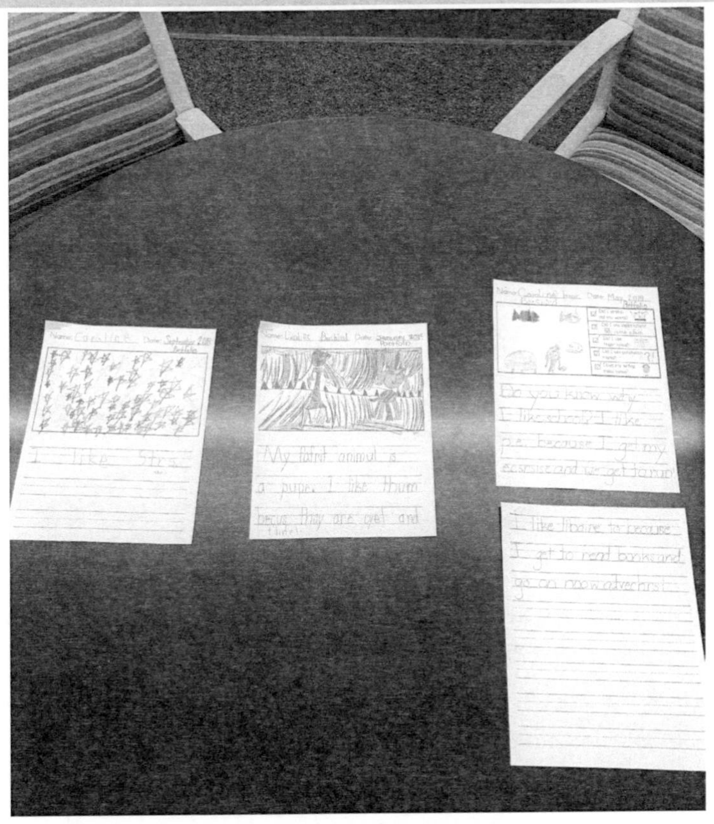

As discussed in Chapter One and Two, the use of work samples to assess student progress is critical for students to accurately monitor and assess their progress. Figure 4.5 illustrates a visual that one student at John F. Long used to assess their own writing performance. Here, the teacher provided scaffolds at the bottom of the page about how to create the piece of writing. He included examples as well as cues (in yellow) for how students can move forward. Correspondingly, the example in Figure 4.6 follows leveled success criteria. This criteria serves as a key support structure for aiding students in self-assessment.

Figure 4.5 *Student Work Samples Aligned to Success Criteria at John F. Long Elementary School*

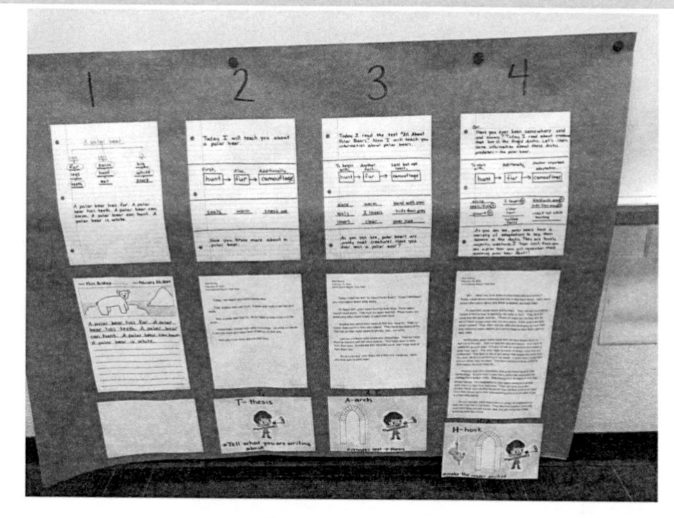

As discussed in previous chapters, when students engage with teachers on the development of success criteria, there is a better chance that students will understand and utilize criteria to monitor their own learning. In the image below, you can see notes and small changes to the learning intentions and success criteria along. In this image, students also self-identified their current performance along the continuum of complexity (surface, deep, and transfer).

Figure 4.6 *Learning Intention with Leveled Success Criteria*

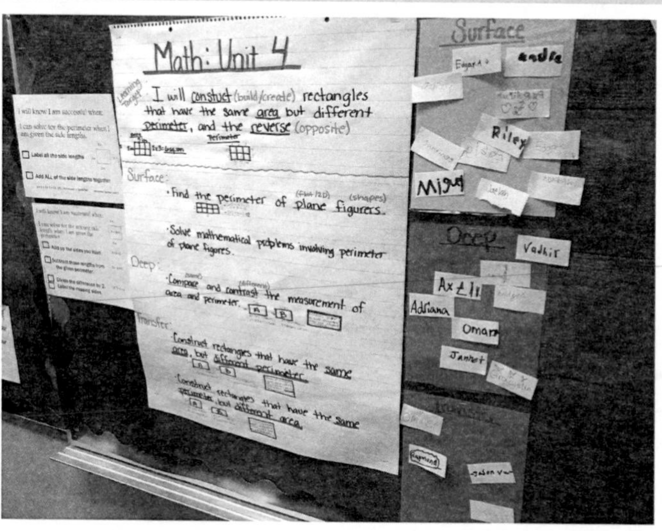

For students, progress towards meeting outcomes, a scoring scheme, is helpful to denote their level of performance towards complexity over time. Figure 4.7 illustrates one version of a four-point scoring scheme that denotes a student's development of surface, deep, and transfer level learning. Following the establishment of a scoring scheme, students can track their progress on a variety of assessments. Figures 4.8 and 4.9 show other ways to track student progress.

Figure 4.7 *Scoring Scheme Measuring Student Progress*

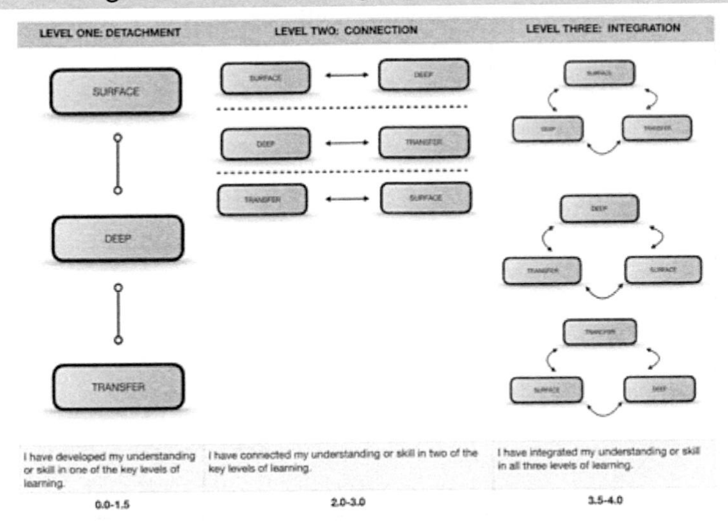

Note: Figure 4.7 shows a scoring scheme for measuring student progress. Please see Chapter Five for a detailed description of each level presented in table

Figure 4.8 *Student Self-Assessment*

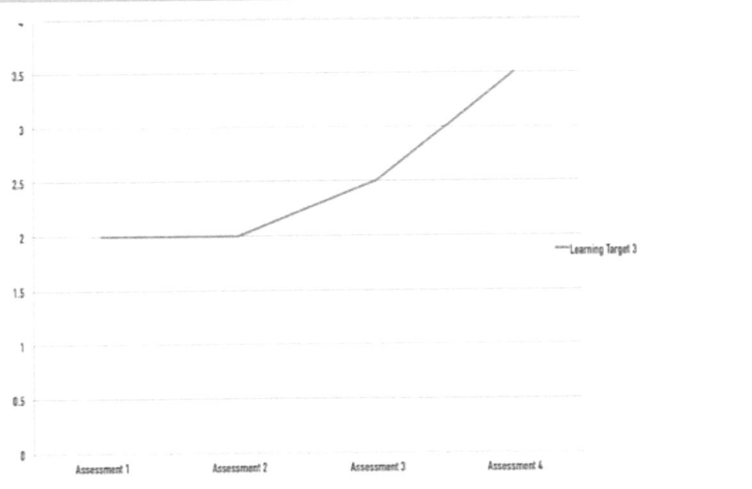

Finally, students can discuss their progress and proficiency over time. The video at www.first eduction-us.com/busyteacher illustrates one young learner discussing her performance.

To see the video, go to www.firsteducation-us.com/busyteacher

Figure 4.9 *Figure 4.9 Progress and Proficiency Matrix Table (McDowell, 2018)*

Practice 11: Provide Multiple Opportunities and Choice for Students to Represent Their Understanding

In *Teaching for Transfer* (2020), I make the argument that a tapestry of assessment tasks should be used to represent student proficiency, progress, and perspective. Imagine students had a portfolio as one way to collect a variety of assessment information to make a determination of their progress and to discuss what strategies worked well for them and what strategies should be discarded for future performance. For example, take a look at the videos at www.firsteducation-us.com/busyteacher to watch as a learner discusses their reflections on their own work and the types of tasks they used to determine their performance.

To see the video examples of student reflection and choice, go to www.firsteducation-us.com/busyteacher

Correspondingly, students should have a degree of selection in the way they prove their competency, showcase questions yet to be answered, and demonstrate growth yet to be achieved. The following video illustrates the power of choice through the student-constructed success criteria and collective decision making. Choice is such a powerful motivator and an essential element to activating student learning. The following video illustrates the power of choice-developing student activation. Here learners are discussing their own unique interests and how they will convey their learning over time.

Lastly, students should have the opportunity to share the key strategies they used to show growth. The video below illustrates how powerful reflections are to students in their development towards taking ownership over their own learning.

Practice 12: Establish Protocols for Discussions, Debate, and Decisions

Collaboration requires interaction between groups of people. Often in academic settings, those interactions include discussing core content, debating on various viewpoints, proposals that link to core content, and decisions that groups make to solve a problem. The argument here is that teachers must structure these interactions to ensure the development of content knowledge and the skill of collaboration. Throughout this book, several protocols have been mentioned for teachers and students to discuss, debate, and make decisions on. Table 4.3 illustrates a number of protocols and definitions. It also shows the alignment of those protocols to discussions, debates, and decisions.

Table 4.3 *Protocols for Collaboration*

Types of Conversations	Protocol Example	Description of Protocol
Discussions	Concentric Circles	One group of students forms an "inside" circle, facing the second group of students in an "outside" circle. Students pair off to discuss a prompt or question, then the outside circle rotates so that students have a new pair for the next round

Debates		Rapid Perspective Debate The teacher will present a question in which students will argue for/against. Students will then gather evidence for two sides of an argument. Next they will pick a side and then meet in small groups to determine the most effective way to convince others. They will then break into small groups to debate each other (2 for one side of an argument and 2 against). Next, the groups will give each group feedback on the strengths and weaknesses of each group's arguments. Groups then go back to larger groups and develop a rebuttal. Next the small groups meet again to present their arguments. Finally, the teachers assign groups to analyze both sides of the argument by focusing on alternatives to both sides of the argument, different perspectives, and different solutions then what both groups presented.
Decisions	Fist of Five	The Fist to Five protocol is used to determine a team's overall commitment to a potential decision and/or to determine if a team is going to move towards a decision. • A fist means, "I vote NO." or in consensus it means , "I object and will block consensus (usually on moral grounds)." • 1 finger means, "I'll just barely go along." or, "I don't like this but it's not quite a no." or, "I think there is lots more work to do on this proposal." In consensus this indicates standing aside, or not being in agreement but not blocking the consensus. • 2 fingers means "I don't much like this but I'll go along." • 3 fingers means, "I'm in the middle somewhere. Like some of it, but not all." • 4 fingers means, "This is fine." • 5 fingers means, "I like this a lot, I think it's the best possible decision."

Conclusion

Developing the skill of taking responsibility over one's own learning (i.e., orientation, activation, collaboration) requires simple, daily routines in the classroom. This work is built off of the credibility of the teacher. It is also demonstrative of the work the teacher has put in to show that they care deeply for students, their subject, and for student-learning the subject. Credibility is when *passion* meets *purpose.* The aggregate of these areas of developing student ownership may, in fact, be the most important factor in enhancing student learning. The aforementioned practices should be considered key habits for all educators.

Next Steps

1. Conduct a focus group with a group of students on the areas of student efficacy and teacher credibility.
2. Conduct a final word protocol on this chapter and discuss key next steps as a team.
3. Discuss as a team the following questions:
   - "Which of the areas of efficacy (orientation, activation, and collaboration) appear to be the most doable in your classroom? Why?"
   - "Which of the areas of efficacy (orientation, activation, and collaboration) appear to be the most challenging to do in your classroom? Why?"
   - "What evidence do you currently collect to determine student efficacy (orientation, activation, and collaboration)? What evidence could you collect? What would you do with that evidence?"
   - "What evidence do you currently collect about your perceived credibility with students? What evidence could you collect? What would you do with that evidence?"

CREATING INDIVIDUAL AND COLLECTIVE EFFICACY: PLCS FOR OBSERVABLE IMPACT

The following chapter aims to answer the following question: "How can we collaborate to improve differentiation in our classrooms?" By looking at research and walking through key teacher habits and practices (Table 5.1), grade level and department teams will be able to work together to ensure that students are growing in their capacity for learning.

Table 5.1 *How can we collaborate to improve differentiation in our classrooms?*

Student Outcomes	Teacher Habits
Students will demonstrate.... • a sustained focus on clarity, feedback, rigor, and ownership over their learning between and across grade level • iterative strategies for improving their learning by constant support from their entire teaching staff.	Teachers will.... • Create and monitor a plan of action for habit creation/elimination • Establish clear expectations of collective work • Script the critical moves of collective work • Monitor and improve team performance early and often.

What the Research Says

In 1949, the Mann Gulch fire was raging in the mountains of Montana. Smokejumpers were called in to ensure that the matter was taken care of effectively and efficiently. This was considered a routine fire until it wasn't. As they were extinguishing the fire, the fire jumped across the valley and headed towards the firefighters. The foreman yelled for the men to drop their tools. Only two of the fifteen firefighters dropped their tools. The other firefighters kept their tools and perished in the fire because they were unable to climb the terrain with their equipment. As

Epstein wrote, "One firefighter stopped fleeing and sat down, exhausted, never having removed his heavy pack" (p. 246).

This same phenomenon happened in Colorado in 1994, when firefighters did not relinquish their tools and died with the heavy weight of their backpacks and chainsaws. As Weick wrote, "Dropping one's tools is a proxy for unlearning, for adaptation, for flexibility" (p. 246). It is the very unwillingness of people to drop their tools that turns some of these dramas into tragedies. For Weick, firefighters were an example of what he learned while studying reliable organizations that clung to trusty methods. He noted that they did this even when it led to bewildering decisions. This was especially true when those decisions were conducted under pressure. How does this relate to teachers?

When we think of a firefighter's tools, we often think of the axe, chainsaw, helmet, hose, and ladder. For teachers, their tools are often routines for starting class, teaching a subject, engaging in assessment practices, and managing a classroom. Teachers develop these tools beginning on the first day of school, where they often have to manage 180 unique students. Teachers are constantly under pressure. They are like firefighters. Classrooms are incredibly complex environments. Teachers are required to continually make immediate judgments of what to do to differentiate their instruction in order to improve student learning and maintain effective classroom management. Over time, teachers establish routines to navigate these minute by minute, day to day situations. Judgments become tacit.

Often when teachers and leaders think that new tools and routines are needed to improve student learning, the focus is on providing new knowledge to educators. It is often the case that teachers already have the knowledge they need, they simply need to improve. They lack the support to implement such knowledge in the classroom. The challenge is actually in the change that is needed in the classroom. The routines, or the habits of practice, that have been formed or shaped over time are what need adjustment. William (2019) stated that it is much easier to change what teachers do when students are not present (p. 171). Teachers can quickly change the way they analyze data, collaborate with others, and engage in professional development. When teachers are in the classroom, changing habits is incredibly hard. Akin to doctors washing their hands and smokers quitting smoking, they know what to do. They just aren't doing it.

Over the last few chapters, we have laid out the importance of developing student ownership and expertise. Ultimately, we want our students to be able to integrate the elements of ownership (i.e., orientation, activation, and collaboration) and expertise (surface, deep, and transfer). We want our students to seek out and determine expectations (i.e., orientation), handle challenging situations (activation), and debate, discuss, and give feedback to others (i.e., collaboration). In addition, we want our students to have the flexibility to acquire (i.e., surface) and relate (i.e., deep) additional information within disciplines. We also want them to apply knowledge and skills across different situations (i.e., transfer).

Integrating the elements of expertise and ownership allows students to have flexibility in engaging in any and all situations. Students can be dropped into any situation in which they don't know what to do and, in turn, figure out what to do by leveraging their knowledge and skills. Of course, this process takes time. Students often begin by developing knowledge and skills in one of the component areas. Figure 5.1 illustrates the general process students go through when developing expertise.

Figure 5.1 *Levels of Integrating Complexity*

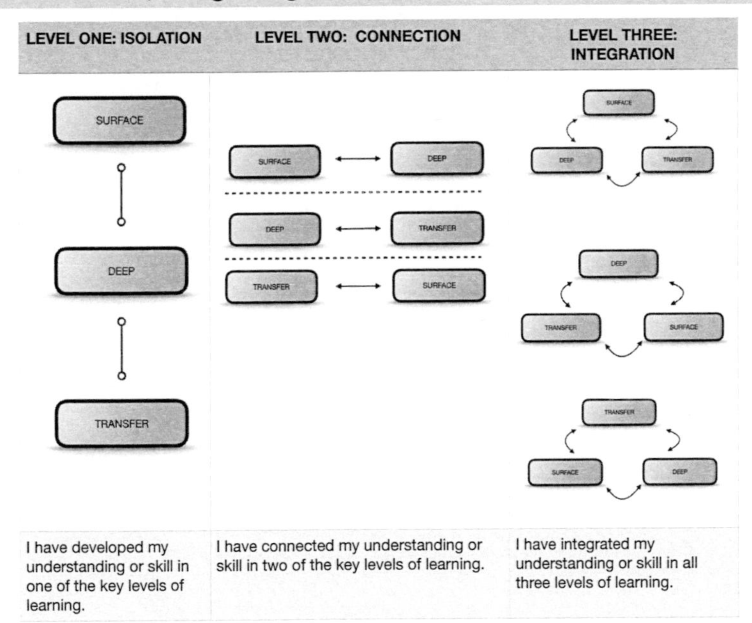

Level One illustrates a student's development of one specific area of knowledge and skill. For example, a student may develop surface level knowledge and skills in understanding the structure and function of a cell. It's possible that this could happen prior to developing an understanding of the purpose behind certain organelles (deep) or where the metaphor of the cell structure serves in assisting the operations of a business (transfer). Over time, students begin to develop a relationship between two of the key components (level two). For instance, students may first experience the importance and use of persuasion. In this example, students are asked to select a topic to debate. Some examples of topics might include arguing for political rights, saving a species, advocating for organic lunches, determining the best show on T.V., or finding a book to read (transfer). After the debating process ends, students can begin to discuss why certain strategies were effective in persuading others (deep). In this example, students are still struggling with surface level knowledge and skills (surface).

Students at level three are able to engage in a complete integration of surface, deep, and transfer knowledge. For example, students began their learning by understanding why artists use their medium to convey powerful stories related to the human condition (deep). Next, students study works of art. They learn key aspects and styles of art conveyed in various pieces (surface). Finally, students transfer their understanding in order to influence people on how to make better decisions using visual representations. Similar to student expertise, student efficacy may follow a similar development process (see Figure 5.2). Our focus is to ensure that students are integrating the ability to know expectations of learning, their current performance, and in planning next steps along with handling setbacks, giving and receiving feedback, and engaging fully in discussions, debates and decision-making.

Figure 5.2 *Student Efficacy: Levels of Integrating Complexity*

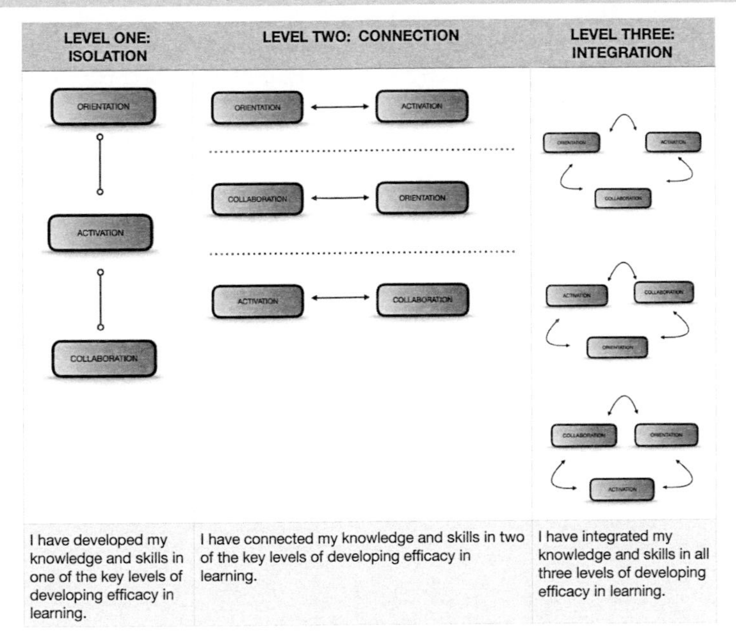

As previously discussed, we want to see our students work towards complete integration of expertise. Figure 5.3 illustrates these outcomes. When developed, students have the cognitive flexibility to solve problems within and across disciplines. Moreover, students are able to find clarity, handle setbacks, and proactively find and solve problems while working with others.

Figure 5.3 *Cognitive and Social Emotional Flexibility: Integration of Efficacy and Expertise*

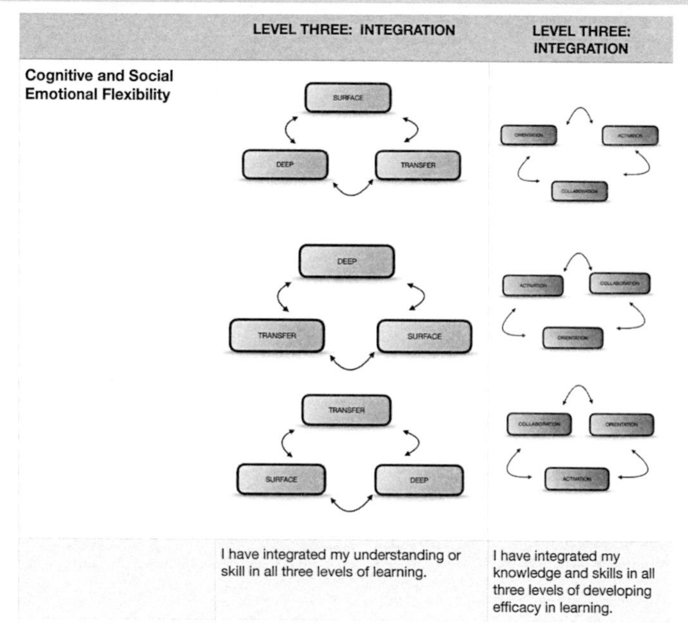

The question is, how do we pick up new tools when they are called for to ensure students are initiating, connecting, and integrating ownership and expertise?

Working Alone

As teachers, so much of the rhetoric directed at us implies that we improve the most when we work with others. Part of the work we need to do should be done together, but a teacher needs to take part in their own individual journey as well. I run every morning, rain or shine. I do this by myself. Part of our work must be done individually. This is on you to do. We need to understand when we should drop our tools (certain habits) and when we should pick up new tools.

Picking Up New Tools: Creating New Habits

As with the firefighters, it is important to recognize the need and have the training for picking up new tools and dropping old tools. Throughout this book, we have discussed the need to ensure that a student's perspective, narrative, and thinking is unearthed and that our decisions adjust accordingly. Before making a change, let's find out if a change is necessary. One way to do this is to collect some evidence of student performance in the classroom (see the Busy Teacher website for more tools for collaboration). Once you find a new habit that you think will be beneficial, focus on integrating it for a significant amount of time (e.g., six months). Table 5.2 provides an outline of the 12 specific practices recommended in this book.

Table 5.2 *Overview of Practices for Each Question*

Chapter	Question	Practice
1	I know I'm doing great things in my classroom, but are my students learning?	**Practice 1:** Discuss successful examples in different contexts **Practice 2:** Create knowledge rich learning intentions and leveled success criteria **Practice 3:** Engage in the co-construction of expectations
2	When it comes to feedback, am I working harder than my students?	**Practice 4:** Establish routines for students to develop accuracy in expectations of learning **Practice 5:** Create routines where students will self-assess and give each other accurate feedback **Practice 6:** Establish routines for students to follow-through on feedback
3	Are our kids engaging in academic rigor?	**Practice 7:** Align instruction to all levels of learning (surface, deep, and transfer) knowledge and skill development **Practice 8:** Engage students in changing expectations, situations, and perspectives. **Practice 9:** Provide pathways for surface, deep, and transfer learning
4	How do we get students to own their own learning?	**Practice 10:** Ensure students are tracking their progress in learning over time **Practice 11:** Provide multiple opportunities and choice for students to represent their understanding **Practice 12:** Establish protocols for discussions, debate and dialogue

Next, we need to find a few ways to make the following practices stick. Based on the work of Clear (2018), the following questions assist in exploring how we pick up and use new tools: (a) How can I make it obvious? (b) How can I make it attractive? (c) How can I make it easier? and (d) How can I make it more satisfying? Table 5.3 provides specific examples of how to address each question.

Table 5.3 *Building Habits, Adopted from Clear (2018)*

How to create a good habit	Example (outside of school)	Example (within school)
Make it obvious - It is clear to you each day that	You have a piece of technology that alerts you to run at 5:00 a.m. every day.	You place a piece of rectangular tape on the floor that you physically stand in when you are about to present to the students in the morning. This box represents your use of 'random calling' with kids.
Make it attractive - You want to do this every day.	You put a short motto on your mirror that says "Remember how you feel, right after you run for two minutes. Awesome!"	You walk students through a fun activity in which students cheer attempts from other students building a stronger culture and removing the stigma of random calling.
Make it easy	Place all of your running equipment near your door for easy preparation in the morning.	You give students process time to discuss their answers and you walk around and listen in on responses to better prepare for how you will start the random calling habit.
Make it satisfying	Every month you meet your goal you pick up a new piece of gear for running, or You go get a slice of "Runners Pizza"	Every week you check on your daily random calling habit and celebrate with a Friday Netflix splurge!

Dropping Our Tools: Breaking Habits

As you review the data, inevitably there will be habits of practice that may not yield the results we want for children. We may, in fact, really like this habit of practice but find that students are not gaining from this experience. For example, problem- and project-based learning may not yield the results we are after when students are engaging in surface level learning. We may need to drop the tool of an inquiry-based methodology during this time. We need to invest in integrating other methodologies that yield the types of results we want. Clear (2018) offered advice for our work of dropping our tools. He posed the following key questions:

1. How can I make this habit invisible?

2. How can I make this habit unattractive?
3. How can I make this habit difficult to implement?
4. How can I make this habit unsatisfying?

Table 5.4 *Breaking Habits*

How to break a bad habit	Example (outside of school)	Example (within school)
Make it invisible	You clip your fingernails every morning so that you are unable to bite them.	When students raise their hands to answer a question you immediately say to yourself "Give us some time to think" outload.
Make it unattractive	You change your language to identify yourself as not using a particular habit. "I'm not a nailbiter" rather than "I don't bite my nails."	Tell the class that multiple voices are critical to learning and if you call on someone without going to at least four other people to tell you in class during the moment.
Make it difficult	You clip your fingernails every morning so that you are unable to bite them.	Use a visual cue on the floor that represents the habit you are trying to form/the habit you are trying to avoid.
Make it unsatisfying	Tell others you are making this change and that they check in with you weekly.	Review exit tickets and find out the alignment between what you heard in class versus what students had written. If there is significant variance, more formative checks are critical.

Once we have identified our key practice and thought through how we will start a new habit and break old ones, we need to create and monitor a plan of action for seeing our intent through to implementation. The following practice is helpful in bringing in new and releasing old habits.

Practice 13: Create and Monitor a Plan of Action for Habit Creation/Elimination

Here you want to lay out your plan of action for building and/or breaking habits. The first step is to collect and analyze data to determine student progress. This is an important step to determine if a change in behavior is warranted. If you need to make a change, then answer the four key questions related to habit change. Next, plan for implementation by going through a set of questions designed for taking action. Finally, you will want to collect data to look at the impact of your changes in practice. Table 5.5 lays out a template for teachers to take when engaging in the work of behavioral change.

Table 5.5 *Template for Taking Action on Habits*

Key Data Points (Pre)	Answers to the four key questions	Lines of Inquiry to ensure success	Key Data Points (Post)
Picking up a tool			
Dropping a tool			

To see all the Busy Teacher protocols, go to www.firsteducation-us.com/busyteacher

One recommendation is to do a bi-annual reflection on your overall changes in practice and the impact of those changes on students (see Table 5.6).

Table 5.6 *Semester Reflection*

What do I know and do now that I didn't when I started?	What have been the major changes in student learning?

Working Together

There are times when teachers need outside eyes to give them feedback, solve challenging problems that elude individual actions, and help make decisions that impact all teachers. Birk and Larson (2019) argued that teachers should reimagine the way that they work together. They argued for a more specific level of implementation of collective efficacy. This specificity can be boiled down to three specific steps:

Practice 14: Establish clear expectations of collective work

Practice 15: Script the critical moves of collective work

Practice 16: Monitor and improve team performance early and often

Practice 14: Establish Clear Expectations of Collective Work

The argument in this book is that you are already super busy and, as such, your purpose for meeting with other faculty should be very specific. The suggestion here is that you are meeting to discuss your impact on student learning. In these meetings, the focus should be on determining next steps to maintain practices that are effective and making changes where data is showing less than ideal outcomes. In other words, the recommendation is to only meet when you are discussing the work of enhancing student achievement. Other than that, send a memo! Your principal and leadership team may establish staff meetings and committees for larger scale district and school objectives, but this will address other needs. Meetings should be governed by student performance data that drives individual and collective decision making. Table 5.7 illustrates three key areas of data collection that may be used to center team discussions.

Table 5.7 *Questions and Evidence to Inform Student Learning*

Progress	Proficiency	Perspective
Are my/our students' growing more than one year in one year's time?	Are my/our students meeting deep and transfer level expectations?	Are we students developing capacity in orientation, activation, and collaboration? Are my students perceiving teachers as credible?
Determining Growth: Evaluating Pre/Post Assessment data	**Determining Proficiency:** Post Assessment Data	**Determining Perspective:** Focus Groups Interviews Surveys

Team discussions should be divided into four specific types of meetings. The types of meetings include: strategic, investigative, capacity building, and check-ins. The more we structure our meetings to specific conversations, the greater chance we will find efficiency and effectiveness when everyone is together. Table 5.8 lays out suggested meeting types, purposes for each meeting, frequency of such meetings, and the duration of time for each meeting. Often teachers have all of these meetings simultaneously. This can create confusion, stress, and boredom. Take a few minutes to determine which of these meetings you are already having and what changes you may need to make in the organization of meetings with colleagues.

Table 5.8 Meeting Types

Meeting Type	Description	Key Questions we want to answer	Frequency	Duration
Strategy	These meetings happen 1-2 a year and enable teams to determine areas of focus for the school year. For example, after looking at student data a team may determine that they want to focus on a specific area of student learning (e.g., feedback) and key practices associated with that area (e.g., Practice 4, 5, & 6).	How do we figure out what are the right things to do for students in our classroom?	1 - 2 per year	120 Minutes
Team Investigations	Teacher teams conduct individual short term investigations into the impact of a new practice on their students and then meet and discuss their work with their team.	Are these the right things to do?	1 per quarter	60 Minutes
Capacity Building	Teacher teams set aside time to share their key learning from impact cycles and work with each other to build capacity. Professional learning may include book studies, conferences, onsite visits with consultants, teacher video vignettes, and debriefing classroom observations.	Am I doing the right things?	1 per quarter	1/month (or more often depending on the needs of the team)
Check in	Teacher teams set aside time once a month to assess logistical matters that infringe on their ability to focus on student learning and teacher practice. These meetings are focused on problem solving and end with next steps that everyone can take to improve logistical matters.	Are we taking care of all the "other things" that are in our way to improve student learning?	Monthly	15 minutes

Finally, once specific meeting types have been established, teams should begin planning when certain meetings will take place throughout the year (see Table 5.9 as an example of a year-long example).

Table 5.9 *Yearly Overview*

August	September	October	November	December	January	February	March	April	May	June
S	PL	C	I	PL	C	I	PL	C	I	S

Practice 15: Script the Critical Moves of Collective Work

To ensure effectiveness and efficiency of collective work, teams should create structure agendas for each meeting type. Templates for suggested agendas for strategy, team investigations, and professional learning meetings can be found at www.first education-us.com/busyteacher. The key here is to script the critical actions for when teams meet. Take a few minutes and review these agendas and compare them to the types of meetings and agendas you have now. Think about how they are similar and different.

Practice 16: Monitor and improve team performance early and often

As teams, work together. Individuals need to ensure that agreements, protocols, and meeting structures are followed with a high degree of fidelity. This does not mean that people are not free to share their opinions and create new solutions. Strategic meetings are often divergent and can be creative, ensuing high levels of discussion and debate. These practices ensure that teams continue to get better at teaming. One way to ensure that these critical strategies are implemented in groups is to establish roles that ensure all team members are responsible for team performance and dynamics. The roles presented in Table 5.10 may be of assistance.

Table 5.10 *Team Roles*

Roles	Description
Process/Structure Role	The following role is designed to ensure that the meeting agenda is implemented and agreements are followed.
Alternative/Perspective Role	The following role is designed to ensure multiple perspectives and data sources are considered when making decisions.
Accuracy/Follow Through Role	The following role is designed to ensure that the team understands the mandate of the work, that information shared is valid and reliable, and that actions decided will be implemented.

Conclusion

To ensure that individual and collective teacher actions enhance student learning, teachers need to inspect their daily routines. When you look at your individual practice, you are primarily looking at habit formation or elimination. Teaching is so complex that you have created tacit habits that have allowed you to manage complex situations and move the needle on achievement. Sometimes a habit needs to be broken or a new habit needs to be added to get better for kids. This chapter walked through a process for doing just that individually and collectively.

Next Steps

1. Establish key personal professional habits you want to engage in and habits you want to eliminate. Using tables to plot a course for habit formation or elimination. Discuss your plan with a colleague and set an expectation to meet with your colleague in six weeks and discuss your status in meeting your goals.

2. In a collaborative group of colleagues, go through this chapter and create a collective purpose, outline the year, review agendas, and identify the forms of evidence that are most impactful for student learning and doable for your team to collect and utilize.

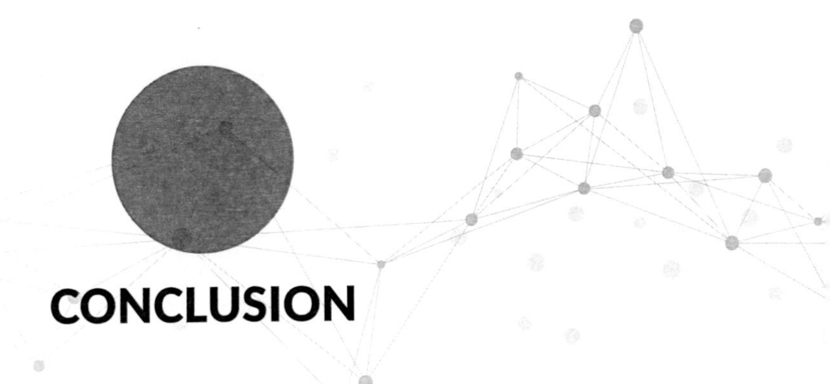

CONCLUSION

If there is one more question that we should reflect on before we end this book it is: Do we need to get better? The science has gotten much clearer on the impact educators have on student learning. It has revealed the variance of that impact given the decisions we make on a daily basis. Teachers have the choice to make a significant difference in the lives of children. Such choices include daily habits of applying certain strategies that ensure students have clarity, engaging in feedback, experiencing rigorous instruction, and developing ownership over their learning. Moreover, teachers have the choice to constantly improve their own learning and work with other faculty to refine and get better. The habits of best practice have also gotten much clearer.

This book has provided a number of approaches that enable teachers to improve student learning. Its goal was to make differentiation doable. We can now break differentiation down into levels of complexity (surface, deep, and transfer) and student ownership over their own learning (orientation, activation, and collaboration). This was followed by tangible practices that we can implement on a daily basis. I know you are busy, so my recommendation is to stay small and stay focused. Pick a key habit of practice. Then, implement, refine, and inspect the impact of those habits on student learning. By doing this you will likely take the good things you are already doing and make them better and ultimately improve student learning.

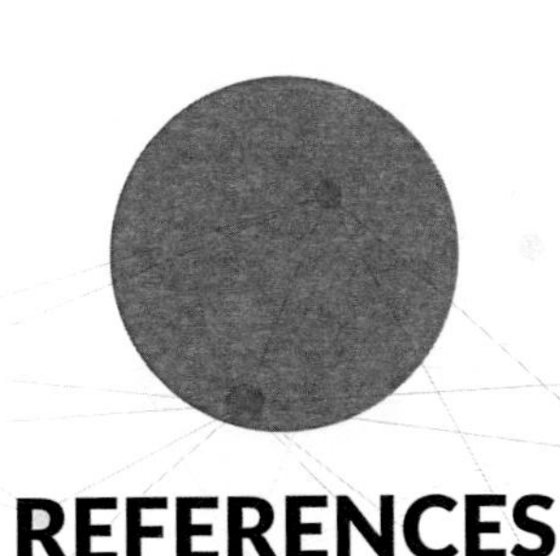

REFERENCES

Beers, K. & Probst, R. E. (2012). *Notice & note: Strategies for close reading.* Portsmouth, NH: Heinemann

Biggs, J. B. & Collins, K. F. (1982). *Evaluating the quality of learning: The SOLO taxonomy*. London, U.K: Academic Press.

Clear, J. (2018). *Atomic habits: An easy & proven way to build good habits & break bad ones.* New York: Penguin Random House

De Bono, E. (1999). *Six thinking hats.* New York City, NY: Back Bay Books

Epstein, D. (2019). *Range: How generalists triumph in a specialized world.* Macmillan Publishers

Gregory, G. H. & Kuzmich, L. (2014). *Data driven differentiation in the standards-based classroom.* Thousand Oaks, CA: Corwin

Gladwell, M. (2019). *The obscure virus club* [Audio podcast]. http://revisionisthistory.com /episodes/40-the-obscure-virus-club

Hattie, J. (2009). *Visible learning: A synthesis of over 800 meta-analyses relating to achievement*. Routledge.

Hattie, J., & Donoghue, G.M. (2016). Learning strategies: A synthesis and conceptual model. *Science of Learning, 1.*

Hattie, J. &Yates, (2014). *Visible learning and the science of how we learn.* Routledge, NY.

Marzano, R. J. (2017). *The new art and science of teaching*. Solution Tree Press.

McDowell, M. (2017). *Rigorous PBL by design: Three design shifts for developing confident and competent learners*. Thousand Oaks, CA: Corwin Press

McDowell, M. (2018). *The lead learner: Improving clarity, coherence, and capacity for all*. Thousand Oaks, CA: Corwin Press

McDowell, M. (2019). *Developing expert learners: A roadmap for growing confident and competent students.* Thousand Oaks: Corwin Press

McDowell, M. (2020). *Teaching for transfer: A guide for designing learning with real-world application.* Solution Tree Press

Muller, D.A. (2008). *Designing effective multimedia for physics education.* University of Sydney.

Nuthall, G. 2007. *The Hidden Lives of Learners*. NZCER Press.

OECD (2016c). *PISA 2015 Results (Volume II): Policies and Practices for Successful Schools*. Paris: OECD Publishing.

OECD (2016d*). Skills Matter: Further Results from the Survey of Adult Skills* Paris: OECD Publishing. http://dx.doi.org/10.1787/9789264258051-en

Recht, D. R. & Leslie, L. (1988). Effect of prior knowledge on good and poor readers' memory of text. *Journal of Educational Psychology*, *80*(1), p.16.

Wexler, N. (2019). *The Knowledge Gap: The hidden cause of America's broken education system--and how to fix it.* New York, NY: Penguin Random House

Willingham, D. (2009). *Why don't students like school?: A cognitive scientist answers questions about how the mind works and what it means for the classroom*. San Francisco, CA: Jossey-Bass

Wiliam, D. (2019). *Creating the schools our children need: Why what we're doing now won't help much (and what we can do instead).* West Palm Beach, CA: Learning Sciences International